No Average Joseph

REFRESHING ANCIENT WORDS

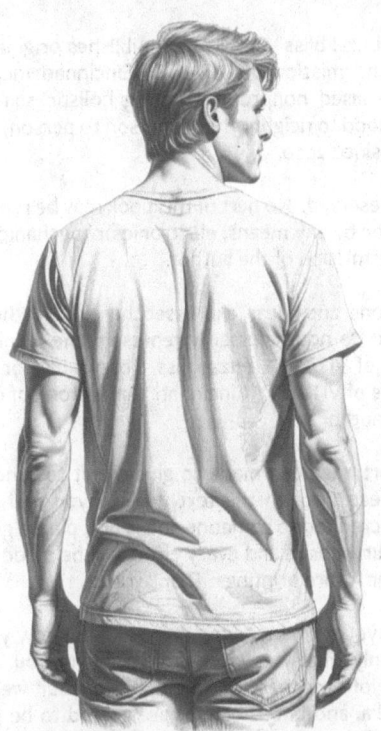

BRIAN J. SHIRCLIFF

VITALITY

buzz, bliss + books

NO AVERAGE JOSEPH: refreshing ancient words
(NAKED LITTLE FICTIONS, vol 2)
updated for the stage edition (2026)
Copyright © 2025, 2026 by Brian J. Shircliff
Published by VITALITY buzz, bliss + books LLC
vitalitybuzz.org

VITALITY buzz, bliss + books LLC publishes original creations to grow the mission of VITALITY Cincinnati Inc, a 501(c)3 education-based nonprofit: sharing holistic self-care from neighborhood to neighborhood, person to person, and breath by breath since 2010.

Every effort has been made to give credit to other people's original ideas through the text itself. If you feel something should be credited to someone and is not, please get in touch through our website and every effort will be made to correct this text for future printings. Thank you!

We invite you to honor your mind, your body, your whole self. Do only what you know to be right for you. While the invitations offered here in this book, on our websites and social media, and in our classes are geared to be gentle and easily modified by the participant to fit the participants' needs, please consult your medical doctor or health professional before undertaking any practices.

ISBN: 978-1-954688-46-9

...to feel even the faintest breeze
as if for the first time...

in gratitude

to the VATRONS
who breathed life into this book
by pre-ordering their copy

to the actors who came together
December 16, 2025 for a reading-rehearsal &
December 17, 2025 for a dramatic public-reading

and to the audience who found the humor and
wisdom in the midst of the tragedy, comedy, and
wild language of this ancient story and shared
such helpful insights afterwards

You are all much loved and appreciated!

dedication

"For this course, you need to attend four plays and write a review for each one," Mr. Hendrick asked of our sophomore English class earlier in the year at St. Xavier High School, the Jesuit school in Cincinnati.

So on November 17, 1989, I went to our school play *The Fifth Sun*, about the life and assassination of Oscar Romero, bishop of El Salvador, defender of the poor. Earlier in the day, we'd all been stunned by the news that the Salvadoran Army had killed six Jesuits, their housekeeper, and her daughter. Like Romero did through his postion as archbishop, the Jesuits had been advocating for the poor from their teaching posts at Central American University in San Salvador.

Theatre Xavier began the play that night with a chilling recording of NPR's newscast about these eight murders. Romero's story became all too real for all of us that night, even more so for the people of El Salvador. Why was this happening? Again?!

Those who killed Romero in 1980 and those who killed the six Jesuits and their housekeeper and her daughter were trained by the US military in what used to be called the School of the Americas, funded with our families' US taxpayer dollars. In 2001, the school's name was changed to the Western Hemisphere Institute for Security Cooperation. Through the decades the school/institute has been allowed to continue by Republican and Democrat commanders-in-chief and lawmakers of my nation, even when it has been revealed time and time again that the school/institute's training emboldens their students to kill the poor and the poor's advocates in the students' home countries. It is one of the many reasons citizens of Central and South America have crossed the US border seeking asylum from the killing squads within their own countries.

I dedicate *No Average Joseph* to Theatre Xavier whose productions inspired me for decades... through tears, laughter, lamentation, wonder, appreciation...often in the same production. Communal lament, as the biblical tradition reminds us, is the key to grieving the past and releasing our grip upon it and all that it 'was' for us—helpful and unhelpful—so that we can then open our palms to a new future.

No Average Joseph is an opportunity for shared laughter and shared lament. May this play revive the biblical tradition and welcome new life and new possibilities that wander around, cross borders, and are available in the breeze, for any and all of us.

a few words of warning

Genesis is a rough book of the Bible. Think about what's in there...

Brother kills brother.

God kills nearly every human and creature with a flood.

Abraham thinks he hears God wanting him to kill his son borne by Sarah...and Abraham very nearly kills little Isaac.

Abraham and Sarah chase off his other son borne by Abraham's mistress because Sarah felt bothered and a rival to the mistress.

Two daughters get their father drunk and have sex with him to be sure they have children and fulfill their ancient duty.

A group of brothers kill a whole town for the sins of one young man.

And there is much rape. Often by unlikely characters.

By the end of Genesis, it's hard to find a hero.

But it does end well. Genesis ends well. And so will this play...though you'll need to take good care of yourself through the sexual violence when you read any of the Genesis tales or this play.

Genesis is fiction...at least most of it. All of it is mythic and therefore likely to be helpful in some way. Yet how dangerous it is when we continue to parade our Bibles through worship and never really pay attention to what's in there. If we're not careful, we're bound to repeat these violent tales unknowingly.

Look around today and it's easy to see....

Joseph is a clever little tale. And tight. There are patterns in the story, quite ingenious ones.

As the story goes, Joseph is the second-youngest of twelve in his family. In the ancient world, in a typical family, that would make him practically meaningless.

In the first mention of Joseph in his story, we learn that Joseph is 17 years old. That's old in the ancient world. He should be married with 3-4 kids at age 17 in the ancient world. But it's never mentioned that Joseph's married at 17. And soon we'll know why...

Joseph is NO AVERAGE JOSEPH....

actors

9-10 needed, in order of appearance,
sometimes sharing roles with similar temperaments

Joseph

Jacob

mob of brothers* who rev their engines loudly
   (though we never see their cars),
   two brothers with significant speaking roles:
   > **brother 1** & **brother 2**

youngest brother

salesman (also plays **warden** & **manager**)

owner (also plays **windstorm** & **jester**)

wife of owner (also plays **Rachel**)

guitarist 1

guitarist 2 (played by a brother)

audience

king's bartender (played by a brother or Jacob)

king's baker (played by a brother or Jacob)

king (played by the shortest and funniest of the
   brothers or Jacob)

*** as we learn in the play, these brothers come from
different mothers, so having them be from a diversity
of cultural backgrounds works well with the plot, and
genderbending is a welcome possibility...and there's a
very good reason none of these brothers is named in
this version even though they are in Genesis*

the set

radically simple stage with one simple riser acting as bed and car and upon which a throne will rest...just actors, words and songs, an overhead sign that changes, and a few props

guitarist 1 & guitarist 2 have many lines, much of it narration...their having a musicstand in front of them with a large binder of their lines and the words HOLY BIBLE visible to the audience could be interesting and helpful in a number of ways, and maybe that binder/BIBLE remains on stage throughout

the play

Act 1
Bordercrossing Empire

Act 2
Prison Sluts

Act 3
Prison Dreams

(*intermission*)

Act 4
Prison Chats

Act 5
Within Empire

could be performed as written (with nudity) or as a "swimsuit edition" or "underwear edition" (characters then being minimally clothed during portions where nudity takes place)

after/words

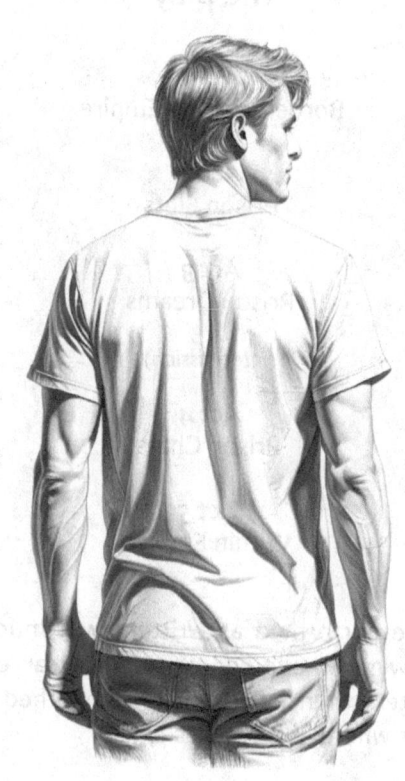

Act 1

under a soft spotlight forestage, an older teen is playing guitar, composing something or at least wondering about something, he wears a white t-shirt and jeans

slowly as the backstage alights as dawn, we can see an older man, sitting behind the teen and staring at him, the older man seems entranced by the teen

after minutes of this, in the distance, offstage, we can hear the sounds of a small mob, engine-revving sounds made obnoxiously with their voices, the revving growing and drowning out the teen's singing/playing

as this mob gets closer and closer onstage, the older man gets more and more agitated, and this revving mob zooms mid-stage between the teen and older man somewhat menacingly with revving/driving sounds, then mob exits

the older two of the mob wear tacky suits, the younger members of the mob wear worn/unkempt professional-casual attire

the teen continues playing/humming for a short time, eventually mob enters again and revs and zooms and stands between the older man listening and the teen playing/singing despite the older man trying to wave the mob away as he continues staring at teen

each of the mob marvels at the way the older man regards the teen, hints of their jealousy emerging

and then a long silence, all exit

— lights fade quickly, then lights up —

the teen with guitar twirls and plays the tune from earlier—adding a few words here and there, trying them out with the tune—he seems moved by something, entranced by something unseen, and he dances with it, whatever it is, as phrases come to him, composing pieces of the song he'll eventually sing (below)

the older man enters, just barely onstage, and observes teen, as teen twirls and plays

the teen begins removing his clothes, as if he thinks he's alone, and his song joins with his slowly, very slowly, finding himself naked there on stage, singing, humming, strumming the guitar, yet never revealing his genitalia to the audience—the guitar every now and then covering his genitalia at just the right time, his naked backside visible

the older man on the edge of the stage seems enthralled by it all, but not so much by the teen's *nakedness as by the whole of it...the young man, the dance, the scene, the song...the teen doesn't know the older man is watching him...*

Joseph (the teen), *singing all of what he was composing earlier:*

> Dancing under the new moon
> The breeze seems my only friend
> The breeze is my only friend
>
> You cherish my real nature
> Nothing have I to fear
> No one have I to fear
>
> You know—you're my true beloved
> You play with me in the night
> Whether we dance or sing
> Whether we eat or drink
> Whether we walk or think
> or lie down and make love
> yeah—lie down and make love
>
> Dancing under the new moon...
> The breeze is my only friend...

Joseph falls asleep onstage, cradling himself around the guitar covering his genitalia

Jacob (the older man) falls asleep too, though after Joseph and nowhere near each other

mob of brothers enters unexpectedly, revving, startling both Jacob and Joseph alike from their sleep as the mob of brothers walks through between them, loudly, one side of the stage to the other, slowly, overly obnoxiously with their revving sounds and zooming through, fake-driving their junker cars

after mob of brothers exits one by one finally, Joseph sits up, still naked, rubs the sleep from his eyes and soon seems to be delighting in the early morning air, breathing in that air as Joseph rolls with it, dances with it, plays in it, all the while Jacob watches, Joseph hums/sings pieces of that tune from earlier

> ...or lie down and make love
> yeah—lie down and make love...
> Dancing under the new moon...

and they sleep again, Jacob and Joseph, separate from each other again, Jacob observing Joseph, Jacob seeming to be in a trance, they then sleep and dream

and in the later morning—the light growing around them, the hum of the earth with the breeze—Jacob moves toward Joseph who is still naked there except for the guitar and asleep on the bare ground

and mob of brothers moves through, loudly again, from one side of the stage to the other, not even noticing the two sleeping there, each one exiting, *except for one of the mob of brothers—brother 2—lingering a little longer to notice the near nakedness of Joseph as the last few of the brothers to exit notices what brother 2 notices but not nearly as long as brother 2 does, Jacob stirs and sees brother 2 staring at Joseph and that seems to disturb brother 2 enough to break his fixation on Joseph and finally exit*

Joseph's backside to the audience, Jacob helps Joseph to his feet, Jacob brings his hands to Joseph's face, head, and shoulders, admiringly

Jacob:
Oh, my boy, my sweet boy, you are so beautiful... just like your mother...and I see It's found you, and you've found It too...the way you dance together... the way It lights you up from inside yourself...

Jacob continues to touch Joseph lovingly, nonsexually, curiously, all visibly to the audience... audience always sees his hands on the teen's shoulders and arms and hands, Joseph's naked backside still facing the audience

Jacob:
but we can't have you parading around here naked—certainly not with your brothers around— they'll—they'll—
(Jacob exits, we hear him rummaging through things off-stage, and he re-enters with an overly colorful dress in his hands)

here, put this on—it'll still give you some room to
feel the breeze you so love on your naked skin—

Joseph:
—but, Dad—

Jacob, *slips the dress over Joseph's head and arms,*
emotionally:
—there you go, there you go—your mother—your
mother would want you to—she—she'd be so
proud—

Joseph:
—but, Dad—it's a dress—I can't—

Jacob:
—no but(t)s

mob revs through, loudly, one side of the stage to
the other, but halts in their tracks at the sight of
their brother Joseph there in a dress, brothers all
laughing and pointing at Joseph, with catcalls of
"fag" and "gay" and "queer ass" audible from them
in the background

brother 1:
Well, would you look at that, our naked dreamer of
a brother all dolled up—

brother 2:
—like the true faggot he is—

brother 1:
—you sure as hell aren't coming to work looking like that—

Jacob, *gesturing to Joseph only:*
—you all know full well he's not going to work with you—not anymore he's not—he's in ecstasy—a prophet's ecstasy—look at him—how he senses the breeze—he—he knows the deep song of life—the life none of you ever seems to have any interest in—always revving through here like a caravan of fools—

brother 2:
—what kind of father are you—always siding with the faggot—you know what God does to fags—you know, you've read it in the Bible—Leviticus!!

brother 1:
—and you know what the Bible says about men wearing dresses—Deuteronomy!!—

Jacob:
—yes—I know—but the near-sighted empire-builders who wrote those laws into the Bible were trying to sideline our kind—us bordercrossers—

brother 2:
—"our kind"—you mean "your kind"—(*circle-pointing to his mob/brothers*)—we here are straight—

Jacob, *kind of under his breath:*
—YAHWEH's love is never straight....

Joseph *to brother 1 and brother 2:*
So let me get this straight—you think I'm a fag because—

brother 1, *lightly pushing brother 2 out of the way and waving all of this away and speaking to Jacob:*
—never mind all that—the real problem here is you never make Joseph to do a lick of work—all he does is write his stupid-ass songs—

Jacob:
—don't you dare demean your brother—<u>your brother</u>—he's a poet—a songwriter—he needs time to develop his craft—with the wind—you see it for yourself—the wind has him—It has him—YAHWEH does—as It once had me, well, before his mother died—

brother 1:
—always bringing up that old bitch—

Jacob:
—don't you dare dishonor your stepmom like that—

brother 1:
—somebody has to stick up for our mother, your <u>first</u> wife—let me remind you—

Jacob:
—I got tricked into marrying your mother—your grandfather—he made me—

brother 2:
—and why don't we get to see our billionaire granddad anymore—

brother 1:
—yeah—why, dad? because you cheated him?

Jacob:
—I did nothing of the sort—I'd made a lot of money on my own in cars—just like you are today—started my business on the side while your granddad made me work for him—and—and your stepmom stole something from him—from your granddad—and we—we had to leave—

brother 1:
—do we get a cut of what she stole?

Jacob:
It was pretty worthless—some silly religious trinket—but—but putting what she stole aside, your granddad wanted to kill me—probably would've killed all of you too—you all were very young—

brother 2:
—granddad would've never killed us—

Jacob:
—billionaires can get crazed about their things— their control on things—they—they always need more—no appreciation for the abundant life in the wandering wind—

brother 2:
—well, if the old bitch would've coughed up what she stole from old grandad he'd have no reason to want to kill us, right? (*lets that hang in the air awhile*) seems a heavy price, doesn't it—for never seeing our granddad again—

brother 1:
—next we'll hear that old bullshit story about how granddad put our dear mom in your bed on your wedding night instead of Joseph's mother—

brother 2:
—maybe heartache's what killed our mom—your distaste for her—

Jacob, *moves closer to confront brother 1:*
—well, I came to love your mom too—even though I was tricked by your granddad into marrying her on my wedding night—I loved your mother—but not like his mom (*points to Joseph still wearing his mother's dress*)—and your youngest brother's mom—(*looks around*) wherever your youngest brother's gotten off to—(*getting angry again*) I don't need you to be telling me about things you never experienced and could never understand—how the whole thing began—how I had to run away from my brother—to save my own life—

brother 1, *getting closer to his father Jacob, despite brother 2's attempts to keep them separated:*
—again, because you tricked your own brother out of his inheritance—and had to run away because

he wanted to kill you too—am I sensing a theme here about you, daddy dearest?

Jacob, *pushing brother 2 to get to brother 1:*
—how dare you—
I'm your father—

brother 2, *getting between Jacob and brother 1:*
—hey, hey, let's not get all riled up—we've got money to make—that bunch of cars got orange-stickers over on Main Street, left behind after last week's nasty storms and now free for the taking

mob of brothers exits, revving and zooming and circling and spraying Joseph with their fake-exhaust as they continue their catcalls of "nice dress, fag" and "queer ass" and "daddy's little faggot boy"

Joseph mouths "so annoying" and then begins twirling around with the exhaust, trying to act unbothered by it, using it, noticing the dress and how the wind gets under it, but after they leave, becoming more and more thoughtful and unsure after all that just happened

Joseph:
See, Dad—I can't wear this—

Jacob:
I know our kind prefers naked wind on naked skin—but you've gotta wear something—especially around your brothers (*says gravely*)—and besides soon you gotta get your songs out into the world—change

things for the better—challenge the Empire's over-reach into our wandering way of life—awaken people to what we can do—

Joseph:
—but a dress? wearing a dress—?

Jacob:
—oh come now, it looks great on you—it, uh, it suits you, right? (*Joseph does not respond*) and—and—it gives you room to whirl around like you love to do, and your mother, your dear mom—you'll be honoring her—her life—with it—

Jacob is overcome with sadness remembering her, mixed with all the anxiety his older sons caused him just moments ago

Joseph, *moving in to embrace Jacob:*
Dad, you know we love you—each one of us—everything you sacrificed moving us all here—even though—even though it—

Jacob:
I knew it would be too much for her—i just knew it—pregnant with your youngest brother and all—

Jacob begins to weep, lights fade slowly as Joseph hums his tune to soothe his father Jacob

the lights come up and they are sleeping apart from each other, like earlier, as they begin to arise,

Joseph is fascinated by the light and the breeze, he gets up and twirls in the light (spotlight) with his dress twirling with him

Joseph, *singing and playing:*

> You cherish my real nature
> Nothing have I to fear
> No one have I to fear

mob of brothers moves through, revving loudly, stops mid-stage around Joseph as he stops

brother 1:
Well, if you aren't going to work with us, you could at least make us some breakfast—

Joseph, *gathering the dress in his hand:*
—if that's some kind of jab about this—

Jacob:
—that's enough from both of you, besides your younger brother here is a prince among men—

brother 2, *laughs:*
—yeah—first princess among fags! (*mob laughs, revving with approval*)

Joseph, *stunned as he gazes back to the light that so fascinated him as he arose, remembering:*
That's so weird, because last night I dreamt I <u>was</u> royalty—an actual <u>prince</u> with gold jewels and

everything—standing there so tall on the hood of an extra fancy car, and all of you drove up in the junkers you all steal—you drove up and circled around me and got out on the ground and bowed down to me—

mob, *a cacophony of catcalling voices:*
Jeeeesussss—
shut the fuck up—
so damned annoying—
stupid ass little brother—
faggot—
queer ass dreamer—
(*mockingly*) oh your majesty—(*angrily*) fucking Empire-lover—

brother 2, *in Joseph's face:*
—so the little faggot now has the nerve to dream— in that dress, no less—

Joseph:
—this is my mother's dress....

brother 1:
Yeah? Well, she's dead—and we never liked her much anyway—neither did any of our moms.

Joseph:
Your mother and mine were sisters, you might remember—and I didn't mean anything by that dream—I—I was just trying to add it all up, you know, making sense of it—like I do in my songs—

brother 2:
—trust me, gay-ass little half-brother, the only sense you make is in silence—

Joseph:
—what makes you think I'm gay?

brother 2:
Um, hun, boys who wear dresses are gayer than shit—and God'll take you down for it—it's in the Bible that way.

Joseph:
Oh yeah, which is gayer? Wearing a dress or actually having sex with the neighbor's son over there under the leafy trees?

brother 2 *gravely, as the rest of the brothers catcall, some of them agreeing with Joseph, some of them defending brother 2:*
Lying down with a man is a terrible sin—don't you <u>ever</u> accuse me of that again—I mean—whatever I do is completely lawful—I never—

Joseph:
—so you're like the preachers who spout out hate for gay-folx by day and then by night are found in bed with male prostitutes—

brother 2:
—shut the holy fuck up—
I'd never do that—not in <u>bed</u>—

Joseph, *laughing heartily, some brothers joining him:*
—just because you stand up to do it makes you better?

brother 2, *ready to pounce on Joseph to hit him:*
I take no pot-shots from a boy wearing a dress—

Joseph, *teasing him:*
—calling me a "boy" might be stretching it—I mean—(*raises his opened palms with the question, playing with brother 2*)

brother 2, *grabbing the edge of the dress and looking under it until Joseph bats his hands away:*
—oh yeah? you wanna show me what you got—

Jacob:
—come now, boys, <u>boys</u>, you know we all love his songs—we all love your brother—Joseph—he's—he's <u>your</u> <u>brother</u>—

brother 1:
yeah, yeah, yeah, him and his stupid-ass songs—come on, guys, we gotta get moving if we're going to get that batch of cars to the scrapper—I mean some of us have money to make for this family.

mob exits revving, brother 2 leaves last as he eyes Joseph and gnaws his fingers angrily and then with some lust/interest, Jacob lingers to make sure mob is gone before exiting a few seconds later in the other direction

Joseph sits there awhile, fiddles with his dress, and

smells it, seems to recall something important, as his youngest brother enters from his hiding spot

youngest brother, *in a much younger voice than any of his brothers:*
I don't like it when they give you so much trouble....

Joseph, *still fiddling with the dress, smelling it letting go of the dress to reach out for youngest brother who sits in his arms:*
Where'd you run off to?

youngest brother:
Where you should go too—when they're all home.

Jacob:
Yeah—I get that, little bro.

youngest brother, *gesturing to the dress:*
What does it smell like to you?

Joseph:
Mom.

youngest brother startles at that, gets closer to smell it, but hesitates until Joseph brings a handful of the dress closer to him, youngest brother is lost in it, as if he's experiencing that scent for the first time, Joseph pulls him in closer and hugs him, cradles him, as he hums a few bars of his song

— *lights fade slowly and they both exit* —
— *pause in the quiet darkness* —

*lights up as Joseph is twirling in his dress and taken
by the light and the air again, he hums his song as
he dances and twirls and is about to lift the dress
over his head and off himself as Jacob enters*

Jacob:

Whoah—whoah—whoah—hold it right there, son,
I need you to go check on your brothers—and uh,
here, take my phone and film them—

Joseph:

—Dad, you know the last time I did that they nearly
killed me.

Jacob:

Oh they won't do that—no—for sure they won't—
they know they'd lose everything they've got if
they brought any harm to you—and you know how
motivated they are by one thing: <u>money</u>!

both pause, laugh together

Jacob:

Compose a little song for me while you're on your
way—and sing it as you go—you never know who
might be listening.

Joseph:

Oh alright, where are they today?

Jacob:

Let me type it in here.

— lights fade, lights up —

Joseph walks with the phone and seems disoriented, scared by the area, can't find his brothers, and hums kind of quietly his song...a rough looking character walks by (salesman)

salesman, *looking Joseph up and down, first upset by Joseph's dress and then turned on:*
Well, um, what do we have here?

Joseph:
Um, sir, did you happen to see a—um—a big group of guys—my brothers—

salesman:
—the car thieves? They're your brothers? Nobody likes them—not in this neighborhood—

Joseph, *timidly:*
—uhhmmm—

salesman, *looking at Joseph carefully:*
—those dudes are your brothers? different mothers, huh?

Joseph:
Four mothers, to be exact—

salesman, *still looking Joseph up and down:*
Uh-hum, your mom must've been the prettiest of the four—and nicest—those boys are real sons of—

Joseph, *nervously:*
—could you just tell me where they are please.

salesman:
Well, they headed out that way—a little earlier than usual—

Joseph:
—thank you, sir—

Joseph exits, salesman turns and watches Joseph walk, regards him with lust, and follows in Joseph's direction (exits)...Joseph walks back on-stage alone and then exits again, lights fall

lights on with mob of brothers passing car dashboard decorations around, laughing, a couple of them counting stacks of money, brother 2 sees Joseph in the distance, keeps staring, with lust

brother 1, *counting out cash and putting it in each brother's hand, as brothers wrestle their way into being closest to him to get their share:*
Pretty good paycheck for a short day's work, eh?

some brothers grunt in approval, some still jostling for their share

brother 1, *noticing brother 2 staring:*
Who do you have an eye for, brother?

brother 2, *trying to disguise his lust:*
—uh, guess daddio sent his little spy again—

brother 1, *seeing Joseph approaching:*
—that motherfucker—

brother 2:
—here's our chance, fellas—

rest of mob, *not in unison:*
what—?
what do you mean?
do what?

brother 2:
—to end daddio's spying so we can get a bigger cut
of the work we do—neither of them work—dad
doesn't work anymore—and that no good faggot
hasn't worked in forever—

brother 1:
—are you thinking what I'm thinking?

brother 2:
Well, there are things I'd like—(*pauses, grunts*)—
let's at least get that dress from him—embarrass
the shit out of him—

brother 1, *mimics :*
"It's my mom's!"

brother 2:
And three, two, one... smile, boys... we're on camera—

brother 1 *to mob of brothers:*
—hide your cash, boys—

Joseph shows up with phone filming his brothers hiding the cash in their pockets, brother 2 wheels around and gets in Joseph's face

brother 2, *looking Joseph up and down:*
Hey there, little half-bro, whatcha doing?

Joseph, *still recording:*
Father wanted me to check on you guys—I didn't want to come—could care less about any of this, or the money you all seem to be hiding—

brother 2, *circling Joseph and getting in his face, ducking around the camera, touching Joseph through his dress, as if to tell Joseph where he/ brother 2 is for the camera but extra feely in spots:*
—hey—I'm over here—and now I'm over here-- make sure you get this—and this—and this—we want old daddio to have the whole 360 degree experience—

Joseph:
—obviously father's suspicious of you guys— probably thinks you're skimming the profits again—

brother 1 in a huff, the others too now on edge

brother 2:
—oh we'll skim a prophet or two—

mob crowds around Joseph and grabs the phone and smashes it to the ground, roughs him up,

mostly playfully like older brothers would with a
younger brother, but sometimes clearly too much,
mob lifts Joseph up onto a car (riser) and circles
around him and pretends to look under his dress...

catcalls from the mob:
oh yeah what you got under there—
good question let's find out—
must be awfully small—
whatever it is—
hey just because he's an alphabet person—
I want to see it—
ain't you never seen it in the shower—it's hhh—

brother 1:
Forget these ridiculous games—

brother 2, *pulling on the dress harder than the*
others:
—but I'm enjoying these games—let's find out
what he's got down here—

Joseph, *in pain from being pulled around:*
—no—<u>please</u>—brother—

brother 1:
—these games end for good—right here—right now—

Joseph *to brother 2 behind him:*
no, no—please—please leave me alone—<u>please</u>—

brother 1 pushes brother 2 away and they skirmish
for control of the situation with Joseph in the middle

but then they seem to have the same idea all at once and pull Joseph to his hands and knees and rip the dress from him awkwardly down the middle and then completely off him as Joseph is there naked and remains there to hide his unchosen nakedness

brother 2:
Now stand up!

Joseph quivers

brother 2:
I said <u>stand</u> <u>up</u>, faggot!

Joseph:
Brothers—please don't do this—<u>please</u>—

other brothers do nothing as brother 2 gets angry and jumps on top of the car/riser and pulls Joseph to his feet, Joseph's backside to the audience, Joseph puts his hands around his crotch

brother 2, *grabbing Joseph's hand, speaking incredibly threateningly:*
Drop your hands or I break them!

Joseph begins crying

and then the wind blows from offstage, catches them all off guard, Joseph calms with the breeze, completely relaxes, stands tall, drops his hands, and stretches his arms bravely overhead

mob, *circling around to Joseph's front:*
Jeeeeesusssss—would you look at that—
I told you he's huge—
yeah, but you didn't tell me he had a, uh, uh,
whatever that is too—

brother 2, *examining Joseph up close:*
— what did I tell you, boys—a true faggot—(*looks
at Joseph's backside, unbuttons his own pants*)

brother 1 *to brother 2:*
—don't you dare—

brother 2:
—leave <u>me</u> be, brother, I just want what's mine—

brother 1:
—leave <u>him</u> be—we won't get as much if you—

brother 2:
—it's just his ass—

brother 1:
—I know—top dollar ass—

Joseph, *standing tall, glaring at brothers, singing
to the breeze as the breeze howls:*

>   The breeze is my truest friend...

brother 2:
Shut the fuck up—I hate that damned song—

brother 2 lunges for Joseph as brother 1 whacks brother 2 to knock him away hard, salesman enters, brother 1 motions for salesman to come closer, brother 1 and salesman whisper and salesman pulls out a wad of cash and gives it to brother 1, salesman takes Joseph by the arm and drives off with Joseph, the rest exit the other direction

— lights fade, lights up again —
— stage is now split —

Jacob and youngest brother sit on one side; on the other side of the stage, Joseph sits in a jail cell, caption above Joseph's side says "EMPIRE"

mob rushes in revving excitedly to Jacob and youngest brother's side

brother 1, *pocket bulging with cash, holding Joseph's torn dress, says to their father Jacob:*
Father, have you heard from Joseph?

Jacob, *frantic:*
He hasn't responded to my texts. Have you seen him? Didn't he—didn't he make his way to you?

brother 2, *angrily, pushing past brother 1:*
Why did you send him to spy on us—

brother 1, *handing Joseph's dress to Jacob:*
—no—no, we didn't see him—but we—uh—we found this on our way back home—do you—do you think it's Joseph's?

Jacob, *becoming more and more frantic:*
Where—where did you find this? Where is my Joseph? Did you look for him? <u>My Joseph</u>!

Jacob brings the dress to his face and weeps and then drops it, youngest brother picks it up and lovingly smells it like he had done that morning when Joseph was wearing it, mob of brothers shoves brother 1 to the edge of the stage until he gives them each a few more bills from his pocket, each brother exits once he gets his money

alone now with his father/Jacob and youngest brother, brother 1 peels off a couple bills from that wad and drops them at his father's feet and exits

Jacob exits next, weeping quietly

youngest brother weeping leaves last holding the dress and looking out in the direction of Joseph on the other side of the stage, the other side of the world, the bills left by brother 1 remain on stage as that side of the stage is empty of everything else

on the other side of the stage, now more brightly lit, Joseph is in a jail cell wearing some dingy jail-rag shorts and bare-chested like the other inmates, owner comes and looks them all over and points at Joseph and gives salesman a wad of cash

owner takes Joseph away by the arm, continuing to look him up and down and smiling

— *lights fade, lights up* —

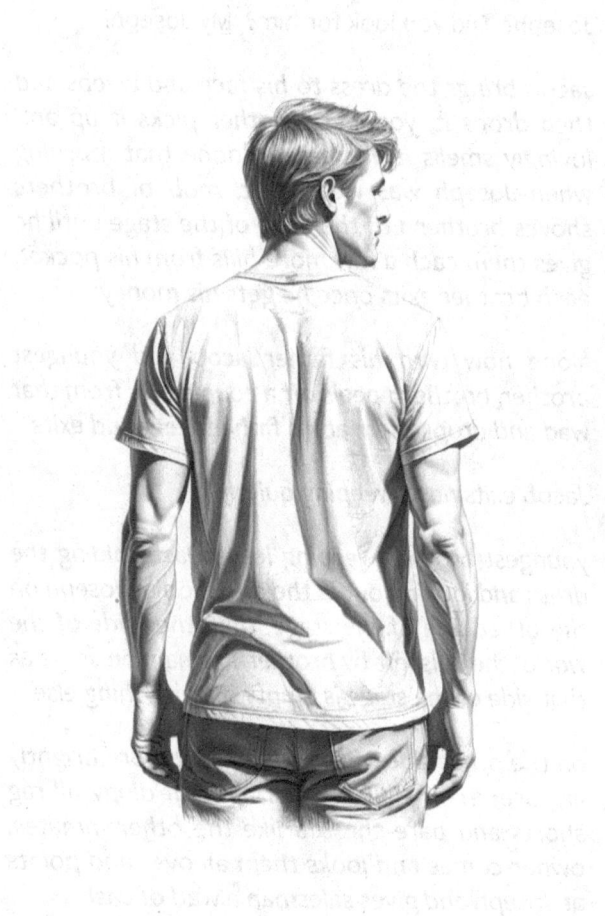

Act 2

EMPIRE sign still there where it was but actors use full stage—in the home of Joseph's new owner and owner's wife

owner, *excitedly/anxiously*:
So this is your new life now—no more prison for my special guy!—you see—I'm pretty special too—and you—you'll manage my house and all my affairs and—uh—show me <u>all</u> you can do and I'll put you in charge—uh—in charge of everything—and (*as an afterthought*)—oh—uh—and this is my wife—

owner exits, wife begins caressing Joseph but Joseph wriggles away and begins doing the dishes and tidying up the place while wife watches and touches herself sexually and tries to allure Joseph, who continues to turn his back in any direction she positions herself in the room, often seductively

owner walks through and stops wife and scolds her, wife exits upset, owner exits the other dirction and re-enters with new garb for Joseph

owner *to Joseph:*
We can't have you wearing prison garb here, the clothes of your old life—here let's take these off you—oh my—(*as he looks at Joseph's naked*

frontside, Joseph's naked backside to the audience)—
oh myyyy—yes indeed—yes indeeeeeed—you're
a man—uh a person—a <u>person</u> with everything
anyone would want—damn yes—you—you must
wear this—especially with my wife around—uh—
here let me help you put this on—here—I—uh—
want to help—umhmmmm....

*owner dresses Joseph in a tightfitting black
bondage/dominatrix dress, revealing an extra
bulged front-midsection*

Joseph:
Um—what was it you said you do again—for a
living?

owner:
Oh—I work for the king—head of the butchers and
executioners—

Joseph:
—that's a strange combination—

owner, *feeling the new dress's sleekness with his
hand before standing and sticking his own backside
into Joseph's frontside and pulling Joseph in closer
and closer to him with straps from Joseph's new gear:*
—I—uh—I protect the king—and to be so close to
the king—he had to take something very important
from me—so with what's left—uh—I—I like sharp
pointy things—I like to—I like to see where those
big pointy things go—how deep they can go—

Joseph:
—uh—uh—oh—I—I—um—see—

owner, *salivating:*
—umhmmm—

Joseph, *trying to change the subject:*
And your wife?

owner, *grunting unhappily, pulling Joseph in tighter:*
What about her? Don't bring her up at such an important moment as this—

Joseph, *panicking a second, then trying a new tack:*
—uh—uh—so now you own me—

owner, *salivating:*
—umhmmm—

Joseph:
—and the king owns you—

owner, *pulling Joseph in closer:*
—hun—in this kind of world—everyone is owned by someone—even the king—(*salivating even more at the thought*)—

Joseph:
—huh? what?—

owner:
—umhmm—what I'd like to do to the king—(*lets go*

*of one strap from Joseph's gear to mimic bending
the king over in front of him and screwing the king)*

Joseph:
—ohh—ohh—I see—

owner:
—get back at him for what he did to me—

Joseph:
—what did he do?—

owner, *snapping out of his fantasy:*
—and one more thing to liven up this little
costume party—(*owner hands Joseph a black S&M
whip*)—yesssss—and you must use it whenever
anyone misbehaves—including and especially your
owner—me—hahahaha—

Joseph:
—wha—

— lights down, lights up, fast —

guitarist 1 *comes out, naked with a guitar covering
their genitals, much like Joseph did earlier, and
they strum the guitar and hum Joseph's song—and
they then stop abruptly and say:*
Now, as the story goes,
YAHWEH was with Joseph,
and It stretched out loyal-love to him...

and then guitarist smiles at Joseph now spotlit not all that far away as Joseph picks up the tune, humming the tune of his own song, Joseph in his new gear twirls around as he does housekeeping work, owner's wife rests on a bed nearby and watches and swoons all over the bed, pinky finger often in her mouth with pleasure, guitarist notices and looks at the crowd curiously before exiting

Joseph doesn't appear to even notice wife and that she is getting more and more naked on the bed as she watches Joseph

wife, *reaching out for Joseph but missing him:*
Sleep with me!

Joseph, *noticing her for the first time:*
Uh—nooo—

— lights down, lights up, fast —

almost an exact replica of the previous scene of Joseph and wife but comedically shorter/faster

— lights down, lights up, fast —

almost an exact replica of the previous scene of Joseph and wife but comedically even shorter/faster, until...

wife:
Damn it to hell—Joseph—please—my husband has

no balls—literally—<u>he</u> <u>has</u> <u>no</u> <u>balls</u>—he's a eunuch—
he has to be—to be that close to the king—

Joseph:
What?!! Gross. What's with you Empire-people?

wife, *getting closer and closer to Joseph before*
running her hands all over Joseph's shiny outfit:
The king has his servants cut off their balls—
to protect the king and his royal family—so I
need you—Joseph—I need you—to give me—
god<u>s</u>damnit—what my husband can't give me—

Joseph, *trying to get free of wife:*
—look here—my boss—even he hasn't known me
yet—and he owns me—you know—
I mean in <u>every</u> way—
and what's in his house—and all that's his—he's
given over to me—
besides him there's no one greater in this house
than me—that's what he told me—and he hasn't
refused me anything yet—you see—not even you
(*screws up his face as if she is gross to him*)—
in that you are his wife—how could I do this awful
thing and—uh—um—dishonor—dishonor THE
DIVINE?!

wife, *as she grabs Joseph and starts trying to kiss*
him and grope him:
Does it look like I give a damn about your honor
or mine? or even if you're gay—lie down with me!

Joseph wriggles free of her grasp but she gets a hold of his S&M tail and wrestles him to ground and strips him with some struggle, he eventually gets loose and runs away naked

wife, *holding the black suit, she smells it, likes it, begins putting it on, gets sad a moment for the lost opportunity, gets a clever idea, and screams, clearly acting a part:*
Rape!
He tried to make sport of me! Look!
Come here and look for yourselves!
His clothes! Here in my hands!
And he's standing outside naked!
You put it together!
Like I did! *(to herself)*
(loudly again) Rape!
That foreigner my husband bought at the prison tried to rape me!

owner comes in, sees for himself, runs after Joseph, grabs him by his ear, and hauls him off to prison

wife *to owner, seeming surprised by owner's response and that her scheme did not work:*
But I thought you'd let <u>me</u> punish him!!!!!

— *lights fade, lights up* —

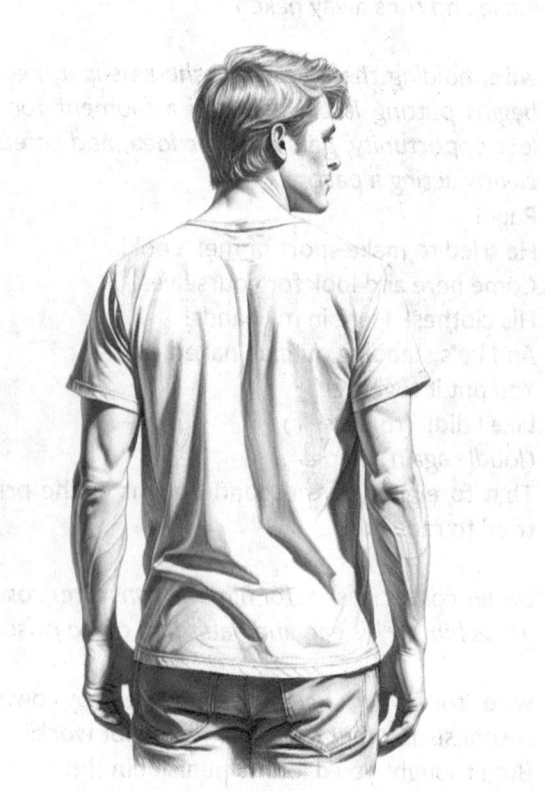

Act 3

owner and Joseph remain on stage where they ended Act 2, guitarist 1 enters

guitarist 1, *strumming, always naked-with-guitar like earlier:*

And as the story goes...

Joseph's owner took him
and gave him over to the round-house—
the inescapable dungeon of the Empire—
the place where the king's prisoners were stuck.

And so it was —
there Joseph was in the round-house, the dungeon.

And so it was —
YAHWEH was with Joseph—
even there in prison!—
and YAHWEH stretched out Its loyal-love to him...
yes, that's right, that's what YAHWEH did for Joseph. (*steps closer to the audience*)
Now if you know Biblical Hebrew—the first language of the Bible— this is all rather curious...
'round'/SaHaR and
'prisoners'/ASYRaY and
'tied-up'/ASURYM
...these are all similar-sounding words in Hebrew...

enough to tie up your tongue saying it all....well, at least in Hebrew....

Not to mention the stretching out of YAHWEH's loyal-love to Joseph...(*laughs, raises eyebrows with curiosity, strums guitar passionately and then lets the sound fade out as Joseph picks up the tune*)

Joseph, *dressed in rags, chest bare, sitting within the prison-dungeon, whistling:*

>   the breeze is my only friend

feeling more and more like himself, stands and sings, dances/twirls, while guitarist 1 plays guitar:

>   YAHWEH, you cherish my real nature
>   Nothing have I to fear
>   No one have I to fear

happier until owner and warden enter and touch Joseph's chest and crotch, Joseph stutters out:

>   Ugh, no one gets my true nature—
>   they fuck, fuck, and fuck me up
>   want me to be their quick fuck...
>   But all I want is to dance and sing
>   all I want is <u>to</u> <u>be</u> <u>my</u> <u>real</u> <u>thing</u>
>   (*extremely frustrated*)
>   —and be who I really am
>   —yeah—be who I really am—

this new verse disturbs his admirers enough for them to exit

Joseph's anger turns to crying quietly and then a long spell of silence

owner and warden re-enter, now more curious about Joseph's tears, depth

guitarist 1:
Now note what happens here with one Hebrew word in our Bible story....(*Joseph and warden and owner try act out everything guitarist 1 narrates but the three actors seem quite confused about what to do whenever one particular Hebrew word comes up*)

As the story goes, Joseph measured up in the eyes of the warden of the dungeon—

and the warden gave into Joseph's <u>YaD</u> all the prisoners in the dungeon—and anything that was done there, it was his doing.

There was nothing that the warden of the dungeon ever concerned himself with that was in his own <u>YaD</u>—
in that YAHWEH was with Joseph
and whatever Joseph did,
YAHWEH rushed upon it, penetrated it.

(pauses)

Yes, that's right—YAHWEH <u>penetrated</u> it—penetrated the situation. Yeah, that's interesting enough but I bet you're wondering what this whole <u>YaD</u> thing is about, right?

Joseph *and* **warden** *and* **owner,** *in unison:*
Yes!

guitarist 1:
YaD is the Biblical Hebrew word for 'hand' — and it's also the same word for 'penis' or maybe even 'phallic-control.' Umhmm. So let's see what our brilliant actors do with these two meanings. YaD #1!

<u>version one:</u> *Joseph is handed over charge of the prison by the warden and Joseph orders everyone around—even warden & owner—to clean up the prison, to smash rocks and produce for the empire—even points to the EMPIRE sign above—but all of it in Joseph's character's style/manner*

Yep, that was YaD as 'hand' or perhaps even 'phallic control.' And now YaD #2 — as 'penis'?

<u>version two:</u> *owner and warden strip Joseph of his prison-gear so he stands with his naked backside to the crowd, owner and warden salivate at what only they can see, warden takes off his own official-warden-shirt and warden and owner slip it forcefully onto Joseph and owner gives Joseph his S&M whip again, owner and warden then get on the ground and start trying to entice an uninterested Joseph and compete for whom he satisfies first*

guitarist 1, *strumming hard on their guitar, anything that eventually comes to a quiet stillness, before continuing:*
And that, my friends, is what Biblical Hebrew does. The multiple meanings of a single word can and will play with any hearer's imagination. And as you can see here, both meanings of YaD—hand <u>and</u> penis—work in the story. A good ancient story, after all, has two tracks running and you're never sure which one is the right track when both work—and voilà—you're left wondering—you're free with your own curiosity. You become the imaginer, the creator.

Now about this whole business of 'YAHWEH rushing upon Joseph and all Joseph did'—that 'rushing' is TSeLeCH, in Biblical Hebrew...

(from somewhere offstage, we hear the sound of the breeze blowing, maybe even the stage curtains move with it) That TSeLeCH word is often used in stories in the Bible involving prophetic-ecstasy, often induced by the wind....

breeze blows even more, owner and warden are cast away from Joseph by that breeze, while Joseph shines with ecstasy

guitarist 1 *strums more, building from nothing to intensity to nothing again:*
Yeah...we'll have more time to talk about that whole prophetic-ecstasy later...

*owner and warden exit, weirded out by the whole
thing...Joseph redresses himself in his prison-rags
and curls up to sleep on a small raised platform
where he is safe to sleep and so audience can see
him...down below him his dream is acted out*

guitarist 1:
As Joseph catches a little rest here, I'd like to
introduce you to a friend of mine from our band
of ecstatics, fellow lover of the wind. Hey there,
friend—

guitarist 2, *entering, also wearing only a guitar:*
—hi, friend—hi, everyone!

guitarist 1, *in conversation with guitarist 2:*
So glad you could join me here. Joseph just put
his head down for a little much-needed rest.
Quite popular in the dungeon. Quite popular
everywhere it seems.

guitarist 2:
In the Bible, they don't call Joseph "beautiful in
appearance <u>and</u> form" for nothing, you know.
(*to audience*) Think I'm making it up? Look it up
yourselves...Genesis 39.

guitarist 1:
Yeah, as the story goes, at least this far, Joseph had
the form that's beautiful to every eye...to men and
women and every human.

guitarist 2:
Well, let's all join beautiful Joseph here in a dream of his own...an experience of one of his ancestors, his own father, Jacob....

Jacob appears down below Joseph in Joseph's dream—Jacob is now a young man, much younger than earlier...Jacob acts all these things out, without the other characters being present (except Rachel eventually), as if he can see the other characters mentioned although we the audience do not

Joseph continues to sleep above Jacob/dream and Joseph does things that anyone in their sleep might do...roll over, reposition, but without trying to draw attention to himself so audience stays focused on Jacob/dream though Joseph's tossing and turning at times responds to the dream

guitarist 2 *tells this long story as guitarist 1 strums quietly in the background in response to the story:*
Well, as you might know, Joseph's father Jacob was quite deceptive as a boy. Jacob's name actually means 'heel-holder' or 'deceptive-one'—or 'over-reacher' or even 'swelling-up.' As we'll soon discover, he lives out all of those possibilities.

As the story goes, Jacob and his brother wrestled in their mother's womb—and Jacob came out holding onto his brother's heel. Recall that in the old world, first boy out earns the birthright, the pathway to the family inheritance.

(Jacob continues to act this all out by himself, often comedically)

But despite being younger, Jacob deceived his father and brother by dressing up as his brother and stealing his father's old-age blessing, the pathway to claiming the inheritance. Whose idea was it in the first place? Who actually helped Jacob deceive his own brother? Jacob's mother. Mother to both of these boys!!

Jacob's brother was ready to kill Jacob, so Jacob's mother sent Jacob back to her homeland for safety's sake. Where was she from? The land of another Empire, of the super-wealthy, the billionaires.

Jacob was nervous...about all of this...but YAHWEH told Jacob it would all work out....

As soon as Jacob arrived in his mother's homeland he fell madly in love with Rachel—love at first sight—

(Rachel enters, wearing a version of the dress that Joseph wore earlier...Rachel never speaks here, but she and Jacob are clearly smitten with each other as they act out comedically everything described by guitarist)

—but Rachel's father tricked Jacob into marrying Rachel's older sister first—and then long after that, Rachel—all of this to get Jacob to work longer for his father-in-law—essentially for free, for these two marriages.

Jacob did his ancient fathering duty with both wives as they competed with each other for Jacob's affections—and babies. But between the two of them, at first, only Rachel's sister was able to bear children. For years. So Rachel had Jacob sleep with one of her own maidslaves to bear children in her name, at least as she thought that would be the case. And Rachel's sister did the same to stay ahead in the baby-making contest.

(guitarist 1 strums guitar seductively when necessary in the background of their story to allow time for each portion to be acted out, though quickly)

There were a lot of babies—good thing Jacob was growing wealthy working hard for Rachel's very wealthy father. Jacob had a side-hustle too—finding abandoned cars where his father-in-law refused to look, out on the edges of the Empire. Jacob fixed up those cars and sold them.

To this point, Jacob had no real children with Rachel—no child from both of their loins—until Rachel finally gave birth to Joseph (perhaps we finally hear from Joseph talking/sounding out in his dream)—the one whose name means 'grower' and 'add on' or 'add it all up' or, rather strangely, 'subtracted one.'

Notice how Joseph has done all of these things or had all of these things happen to him so far in the story...while Joseph's <u>adding it all up</u> and being in-charge in the prison, in more ways than one, the way he got there was to be <u>subtracted</u> from his own family—and <u>subtracted</u> from the owner and the owner's sex-crazed wife's household.

guitarist 1:
Sure seems owner subtracts Joseph from his wife's grabby hands—but maybe it was a move to ensure owner could have Joseph all to himself without his wife getting involved...or at least he shares Joseph with the prison-warden...both of these royal eunuched officials appreciative for how Joseph can '<u>grow it</u>.' No testicles on these royal-serving men—warden & owner—no testosterone, but a prostate and an ass that still feels and still works, no? (*guitarist 1 strums hard on the guitar*)

guitarist 2:
Well, Jacob—Joseph's father—was growing not only in family-size but in wealth there in his father-in-law's house—while Rachel's brothers were growing increasingly jealous of Jacob. They were very lazy and hated Jacob as they rested on their billionaire father's laurels—no laurels they ever earned themselves.

So Jacob rounded up his family and the wealth he had earned and headed out. His father-in-law followed tight. Panicking, Jacob sent word to his own brother that he was coming back home very wealthy and ready to pay his brother for all the wrong done when they were boys.

Through his whole life, YAHWEH had been sending messages to Jacob—through dreams, through the wind—that everything would be alright, that YAHWEH Itself would be with Jacob.

After all, YAHWEH is the wind who breathes us all into life....(*the breeze blows from offstage, stirs curtains at end of stage too for a few seconds*)

And yet here is Jacob panicking—Jacob now caught between two men who want him dead, or at least caged in...his own father-in-law and his own brother.

And there's a reason Rachel's father was chasing after Jacob—Rachel had stolen something important from her father. Of course her father didn't know his own daughter had done that, and probably figured it was his financially crafty son-in-law Jacob who—from his viewpoint—had been pilfering what was valuable to him all those years. But all those years Jacob was working, earning, growing, and even finding old discarded cars in the wilderness—far from Empire—where his wealthy father-in-law did not care to look, or didn't bother.

Now Rachel—she hid her father's valuables underneath her—she sat on them in the front seat of one of Jacob's cars—and when her father caught up to them and searched through everything, her father didn't find what was stolen. Like Jacob, Rachel was quite deceptive. Seems to be a common trait in this family....

Just then, Jacob learns that his brother is coming at him—with 400 men. Probably not a welcoming party! Talk about terrified!

And where is Jacob? In a place known for wild storms that come out of nowhere, near a creek-bed that seems all calm and easy to drive over but can rage to deadly flood-stage in an instant...a creek named Devastating-and-Demoralizing!

All of this as night was descending.
In a wild world away from city lights.
Darkness a car's headlights could barely penetrate.

Spooky. Terrifying. And potentially deadly.

Jacob panics. He divides all his wealth and his family into four groups. Puts the kids born with each maidslave or wife and their own kids in some cars—each little caravan with some gifts for his angry brother—so that if and when his brother comes, perhaps the gifts will sweeten his sour brother and calm him down—and at the very least slow down his brother so Jacob could potentially get away.

And Jacob instructs each gift-group to say, "These cars are gifts for you! Jacob is in the next group!"

Jacob puts Rachel and young Joseph and some more gifts in the last group—to protect his most precious.

Not showing any trust here in YAHWEH's promise of protection, Jacob plans to hide out in the back—behind the last group—behind all of his wives and children!

Jacob takes his family and all that was his and crosses them over the creek-bed. And in the middle of the night, as everyone is sleeping, Jacob crosses back over that dangerous creek-bed—in the darkness of night—and Jacob stays there all by himself...

(*eerily quiet except the faint sound of the wind—slowly building in intensity—and then suddenly*)

—and some random man kicks up the dust and wrestles with him—

(*windstorm enters, dressed loosely in a big strip of cloth that gets wrapped around Jacob in their wrestling, every now and then a wisp of the cloth hits sleeping Joseph causing Joseph to whimper*)

until dawn—

and seeing he wouldn't be able to hold his own against Jacob—this random guy groped Jacob's thigh and genitals—his asshole—

and Jacob's asshole was impaled in kicking up the dust and wrestling with him—devastating and demoralizing him! That random fucked Jacob—penetrated him with passionate, aggressive sex!

(*guitarists allow some time for this to play out, with pleasure-moans and pain from the windstorm and Jacob wrestling, and dream-grunts and whimpers from Joseph...maybe no guitar-strumming*)

But then Jacob found a way back on top....

windstorm:
Let me loose—dawn's climbing up in the sky!

Jacob:
No, I won't let you loose—
until you give me the blessing—
until you bring me into abundance!

windstorm:
What's your name?

Jacob:
Jacob!

windstorm:
No, not Jacob—
you won't be called that anymore—
instead—you are to be called On-Top-of-God!—
because you've been topping God and people
and have held your own!

Jacob:
What???! Please—tell me your name!

windstorm:
Why this—why do you ask for my name?!

guitarist 2, *as guitar 1 resumes strumming guitar in background as Jacob shakes off the cloth and windstorm is nowhere to be seen:*
Just your typical story of God having wrestling-sex with a human...
(*waits*)
I know it seems so surprising for prudes living in the 21st century but this kind of thing is actually quite common in ancient cultures. Know much about the Ancient Greek myths? Zeus has sex with just about every human he sees....

I mean, what's it like to realize here today/tonight that YAHWEH is penetrating <u>you</u> into life—no matter if you "dance or sing, eat or drink, walk or think"—with every breath you take...?

YAHWEH is seducing you right now....

guitarist 1, *pauses guitar-strumming to ask rhetorical questions of audience:*
Have you allowed God into your life—like this?

You sure you're doing what the Bible asks?

As God asks of you? (*laughs, strums hard*)

guitarist 2:
And God offered Jacob the abundance of life,
right there. And the sun shone brightly on Jacob—
as he and his family bordercrossed on through—

(*Jacob and Rachel march on, acting out the journey*)

even though Jacob had been ribbed—sore and
limping—<u>swelling up</u>—like the other meaning of
his name—because of what had happened to his
thigh and ass and genitals—on account of the
devastating and demoralizing wrestling match.

*Jacob and Rachel walk over to Joseph, who is now
entangled in the webs of windstorm, of the dream,
Joseph unsettled by the dream and still within it*

*Jacob and Rachel lovingly soothe Joseph as if their
hands are the gentlest of breeze combing their
hands from head to toe in the space just above
Joseph's body...he whimpers and calms, they stand
aside Joseph and admire him and look to each
other and kiss with much affection/passion and
joyful tears before they exit*

*Joseph begins stirring awake, weirded out by
the strands of windstorm still on him, eventually
shaking off the sleep and windstorm's strands, he
sits up and stretches and stands and eventually
twirls he feels so good*

*guitarist 2 smiles at guitarist 1 and they touch each
other affectionately before guitarist 2 exits in silence*

guitarist 1, , *strumming guitar soothingly:*
Jacob's story of wrestling with and getting fucked by YAHWEH—is that story in your Bible?

Oh no? Oh yes it is. Yes it is.

But the scholars translating the Hebrew Bible from Ancient Hebrew into English or into any language were likely too embarrassed to put out that during the wrestling match YAHWEH had planted Its wispy, sexy seed into Jacob, fucked him right there in the hollow hole and hallowed hole between this thighs and his genitals...to give birth to a new kind of bordercrossing, gender-bending, shape-shifting, happy-to-be-wandering people....

This is an origin story for the Bible's prophets, the ecstatics, here with this ecstatic, song-loving son Joseph, who like the prophets—the ecstatics—likes to get naked with the wind... (*lets the final strum linger, guitarist 1 exits*)

Joseph, *twirling, playing with the long strip of cloth from the Jacob-wrestling dream, removing the rest of his clothing except for the cloth, and singing:*

> Dancing under the full moon
> into this wilder dawn
> into this wider dawn
>
> You cherish my real nature
> And breathe me into life
> And breathe me into life

two new prisoners enter the stage, both of them dressed as royal attendants, though a little roughed up, they begin talking to each other—as Joseph sees them he panics and finds his prison-garb again and drops the wind/cloth which gets pulled off-stage slowly, comedically

king's bartender:
You here too, eh?

king's baker:
Yeah, pissed off our dear doggy-style-loving daddy-king again by putting too much salt in his favorite bread—(*king's bartender laughs*)—and then he had the nerve to crack off about my not being willing to please him on his hands and knees—(*king's bartender laughs loudly*)—I know, absolutely ridiculous—the guy who took my testicles wants <u>me</u> to fuck <u>him</u>—

king's bartender:
—hey hun, we all have our fantasies—(*muses with the idea*)—and nowadays there are strap-ons you can buy that pleasure you both—

(*both prisoners laugh, Joseph comes into their view, barechested with rags, his usual crotch bulge*)

well, well, well, what do we have here?

Joseph:
I'm Joseph, I uh, I help run the dungeon here.

king's baker, *looking him up and down and salivating:*
I bet you do, hun, I bet you do. You can help run
me any day—

king's bartender:
—Joseph. Joseph?! Your name means <u>Grower</u>, ya?

*king's baker & king's bartender both look at each
other and then at Joseph's well-endowed crotch
and then back to each other and laugh as each puts
a finger in his own mouth in pleasure as they steal
glimpses of Joseph*

Joseph:
—well, uh, let's get you checked in—the warden will
want you wearing these shirts instead of those—

king's bartender:
—hey what's a fashionable eunuch or two gotta do
to get some decent clothes in this hellhole—

Joseph:
—rags are the new style—

king's baker, *hitting king's bartender to shut him up:*
—yeah, royal-bartender, rags are the new style!

*king's bartender & king's baker take off their royal
shirts and put on raggedy shirts given to them by
Joseph as warden and owner enter seeming not at
all interested in king's bartender & king's baker but
very interested in Joseph*

warden:
When's showerrrrrr time, Joseph? huh? come on!!

king's baker & king's bartender, *in mock-surprise:*
Lordy—lordy—all the king's so-called men—

Joseph:
—we'll have time for showers later, warden—

warden and **owner,** *in unison, like toddlers:*
—shower nowwwww!!! shower nowwwww!!!

Joseph, *with authority over the king's staff:*
I said <u>later</u>!

— *lights fade, lights up* —

king's bartender, king's baker, Joseph, and warden are asleep, warden kind of close to Joseph, his backside aimed at Joseph and getting closer by the second, Joseph awakens from the sound of movement, Joseph moves away and tries to sleep again—shortly later, Joseph awakens first and soon twirls around humming his tune joyfully and king's bartender & king's baker wake up looking grumpy

Joseph:
What's up with your bad faces today?

king's bartender:
I had the strangest dream—
and I highly doubt there's anyone down here who can interpret it for me—

Joseph:
—oh—come on—dreams are divine—
add it all up for me—
(*king's bartender laughs at the idea*)—
go on—try me—

king's baker, *cozying up to Joseph as warden does the same, both of them competing for Joseph's affections, Joseph shaking them off:*
—yeah—let him try—let him try!

king's bartender, *acting out his dream seductively/ sexily with the king in mind:*
In my dream—listen to this!—
a vine—
right there in front of me!
And on the vine—three branches!—
and it—when the vine—
when it was growing—budding—
the blossom climbing up and out—(*his hand coming out through the fly/opening from inside his pants*)
the cluster of grapes boiling up—ripening—
and the king's cup (*acts like it's the king's ass*)
was—was—
was lowered onto my YaD—
I mean into my hand—
I mean onto my YaD (*uses his hand like a long penis/ erection*)—yes—yes—
and I took the grapes—
and I squeezed the juice right out of them into the king's cup—
(*orgasmically, and then a little embarrassed, he all the*

sudden snaps out of the dual meaning of the story)
and I—I put the cup into the palm of the king—
and that was that—I woke up.

warden and king's baker are stunned to silence by
the bartender's dream and his wildly acting out his
dream, though Joseph is not fazed at all by any of it

Joseph, *twirling and twirling with the images and*
speaking with a fake-dramatic and magic-like voice
as he draws his hands towards himself as if to bring
the interpretation closer with confidence:
Here's how it opens up—the interpretation:
Three branches are three days—
that's what they are!
Within three days, the king'll lift high your head!
He'll make you return to your position!
You'll put the king's cup into his hand
just like the previous right-way
when you were his drinking-guy—
yes—yes—<u>yes</u>!!!—
(changing his tone from his fake-dramatic to one
of seriousness, begging)
now I say all of this—
because if you remember me—
I mean—when it all goes well for you—
please do me some loyal-love—
remember me to the king
and get me out of this dungeon—
you see, I was stolen—stolen away—
from the land of the Bordercrossers—
those who wander outside Empire's reach—

I was forced here into Empire—
and even here I haven't done anything that they
should put me in the pit!

king's baker, *inserting himself between king's
bartender and Joseph:*
Oh hun, I'd never forget you—
so how about my dream—huh—give me a good
interpretation like the bartender's—
in my dream—listen here!—
(*kind of like he's making it up on the spot*)
there were three baskets full of white—
yeah—uh—umm—white—white stuff—
on my head—yes—the white stuff was on my head—
and in the uppermost basket was all the food the
king had made—
he'd been—uh—baking—
the king had been baking—
and birds were eating the white—
uh—the white—the white <u>loaves</u>—
from the basket
on top of my head!

Joseph, *kind of bored by this fake dream, and
speaking with less magic voice than he had with
bartender's interpretation:*
Here's how it opens up—the interpretation:
Three baskets are three days—that's what they are!
Within three days,
the king'll lift high your head—
from the rest of yourself—
he'll hang you from a tree—
and birds'll eat your flesh!

guitarist 1 *re-emerges with guitar, strumming every now and then as Joseph stands by and watches and bartender & baker act out what happens to them:*
And so it was —
on the third day the king hosted a feast with wine for all his high-end subjects—and he needed his eunuchs he'd thrown in prison to serve the feast. And he sure lifted both of their heads—though differently.

The king returned the bartender to his drinking position—the bartender put the cup into the king's—ahem—hand again.

And as for the baker—
the king hanged him.

That's right. Just as Joseph said would happen.

But the bartender—even though he lived—
the bartender didn't remember Joseph as Joseph had asked him to do to the king.

The bartender forgot about Joseph...

(baker remains dead on the floor, bartender exits, Joseph sad and alone in prison, twirls every now and then, but not with the excitement he once had)

...until the king started having dreams of his own... and just so happens no one in the king's court was brave enough to want to interpret the king's dreams.

king's bartender, *sneaking around the stage-curtain from offstage and calling out:*
Joseph! Time to get you all cleaned up to see the king...!

Joseph stands center-stage facing away from the audience as king's bartender and warden come kneel at Joseph's sides, owner standing at attention nearby, king's bartender and warden strip off Joseph's prison-rags, Joseph's naked backside visible

— lights fade, lights up —

empty stage, guitarist 1 walks out naked as usual with guitar covering genitalia

guitarist 1, *strumming guitar quietly:*
Well, my friends, that's the end of Act 3—kinda wild, huh?

And Act 4 is actually ours—yours and mine—before Joseph appears all gussied up as the king likes his ecstatics—

the tale continues—in a little bit—

we're going to have a little intermission here in a few minutes—there will be refreshments and restrooms and all our modern goodnesses—but first I'd like to take opportunity to share a few things with you...and invite your participation....

That famous musical about Joseph—they got some

things right for sure—that Joseph and any prophet worth their salt delights in music, whether that music comes from one of these (*strums guitar*) or the sound of the breeze through the trees or through one's mouth or nose, (*laughs*) through any of one's hallowed holes, in that wild Jacob story.

It's the breeze—the wind—the atmosphere—that keeps us alive, right?

The old Shasu thousands of years ago were thought to be the first people to honor the breeze with a form of the name many of us still use today: YAHWEH.

YAHWEH.

Why 'YAHWEH'? Well, say it out loud to yourself a few times. Go on—it won't kill you. (*pauses, smiles*) That's right, sounds like that breeze through the trees a little bit, huh? Or the sound of breathing, of air vibrating your nostrils or your throat? It's no wonder the ancients got wise recognizing the very the wind as godly, as God, as THE DIVINE—with a name sounding like the wind—YAHWEH.

That's not really mentioned in the famous Joseph musical, huh? Barely mentioned in our modern Bible translations either. But it's there in the Hebrew when we say it out loud.

The YAHWEH-celebrating Shasu people were nomadic, slipping away from the reaches of the great—and deadly—empires to the north and south of their day. Or using those empires to make a buck every now and then.

Empire...such a deadly human-made game. It's the very opposite of freedom with YAHWEH on the open road that any ecstatic knows and craves. (*strums guitar a bit*)

You see, the word 'prophet'—NaBY (*naabee*)—actually means 'ecstatic.' That's right—that's why Joseph was a-twirling away in ecstasy earlier—something that required no special prayers and no special worship places and no priests or rabbis or imams or ministers of any sort.

Maybe you can see why biblical editors and religious people today continue to cover over what's happening in the Ancient Hebrew of the Bible stories about Joseph.

Maybe you can see why the law-writing priests outlawed such ecstatic things like men wearing dresses and men having sex with men—particularly outlawing men being on the ecstatic receiving end of sex. But note well what YAHWEH did to Jacob... <u>JACOB</u>! (*strums and sings...*)

> and lie down and make love
> lie down and make love

(*strums fast and strong*) And then there's that whole thing with the dress.

The dress, the dress, the dress—the big thing they missed in that other famous Joseph musical was the whole business of the dress that Joseph's dad gave him. People want to call it a "coat of many colors" or whatever but the letters in Hebrew say way more than that. CaTeNeT PaSYM (*pass-eem*)—those are the words in Biblical Hebrew.

And what do those words mean?
"Disappearing dress."
"Vanishing dress."
"Shimmering—<u>maybe</u> colorful—dress."

Those possibilities are closer to what's there in the Hebrew.

And does that shimmering dress ever get disappeared or vanished from Joseph...!

Now some of you are probably thinking "well, maybe 'dress' just means what you wear or something like that." Umhmm. Not quite. The only other time we get CaTeNeT PaSYM in the Bible is describing what David's daughter Tamar wore in 2 Samuel 13...a princess dress worn by the virgin daughters of the king. Rather curiously, David's daughter's dress gets vanished from her too—as her brother rapes her.

Think I'm wrong ? Well, look it up...2 Samuel 13. (*strums*)

So Jacob gives his teenage <u>son</u> Joseph a princess dress virgins wore...and Joseph too gets stripped by his brothers as his dress is vanished from him.

What are you going to do, huh, when the Bible has a law forbidding males being passive in sex with males or anyone, when the Bible forbids men or boys wearing dresses...AND when the same Bible also has a story about YAHWEH forcing sex upon Jacob and Jacob climbing on top of YAHWEH to return the, um, favor...<u>AND</u> the famous Jacob giving his teenage son a dress?

(thrashes at his guitar a few licks before soothing it out with...)

The wind is my only friend

Well, I'm sure you have a lot of questions and insights to share, and after about fifteen minutes for us all to water-in and water-out, we'll come back here and have a little conversation before we pick up the story again with Act 5 and discover just what happens with our dear Joseph this time...

just one more thing...what do you think he'll wear in front of the king based on what you know already?

guitarist starts playing guitar more loudly and humming Joseph's tune and backs away into the darkness of the stage before house-lights slowly come on for intermission

Act 4

— after ample time —
— lights flutter, lights up —

guitarist 1, *entering and playing while talking:*
Well, hope you had a nice little rest—saw some of you scurrying to look things up in the Bible—(*laughs*)—well, that's fine, mighty fine of you.

(*plays a few licks from some Summer of Love song*)

Some of you here might remember that there was a day not all that long ago when a bunch of random musicians crafted songs they snatched from the wind—songs of revolution—songs throwing off all the old empires of domination in favor of love...

(*plays a few more licks, smiles*)

"TURN ON, TUNE IN, DROP OUT!" 1967.

This was a toppling not of governments or political parties or corporations or religions. This was a toppling of <u>systems</u>—deep-seated philosophies—in which we all participate and contribute if we're not careful. These are systems of controlling each other through our governments or parties or corporations or religions—even through our families, especially when everyone is of adult age.

The Summer of Love was a first step of dropping out of these systems of control.

The Summer of Love was a revolution—a revolving back before these systems crippled human life.

And how could such a revolution work—back then or now? How?

Through love.... (*plays a few more licks, smiles*)

Psychedelics led the way in the old Summer of Love. But honestly the wind is enough...for anyone who can feel. Even when war thickens the air.

(*plays a few more licks, smiles*)

Well what questions or insights do you have about all that's gone on here today/tonight, go on shout them out, let's not be bashful...

(*if audience is bashful*)
come on now, YAHWEH certainly wasn't bashful wresting Jacob...(*laughs*)...and creating a whole line of ecstatics...those who get high on the wind and let the wind rule...then and now...ecstatics who <u>live into the questions</u>....

guitarist listens and then repeats the insight or question from the audience-member and responds only by playing a few bars of any well-known song from the era of the Summer of Love , any 1967 song in the air that might have something to do with the insight/question and then guitarist entertains another question/insight and responds with a few bars/lines of a different song again in response...

for instance:

guitarist 1:
How about another question or insight?

audience member:
What's Empire?

guitarist 1:
Ah, thank you for that. *(plays the intro bars of "For What It's Worth" by Buffalo Springfield and sings:)*

> **"There's something happening here**
> **But what it is ain't exactly clear**
> **There's a man with a gun over there**
> **A-telling me I got to beware..."**

How about another question or insight?

to prepare, it might be best for guitarist 1 to have about ten Summer of Love/1967 songs in mind and just play a few bars/lines of a song in response to any question/insight from an audience member...

guitarist 1's song-responses could be profound, silly, or entirely random....

<u>Bands who played at the 1967 San Francisco Be-In...</u>
the "Gathering of the Tribes" to unite the hippie movement...

   Jefferson Airplane ("Somebody to Love")
   Grateful Dead ("Morning Dew")
   Big Brother and the Holding Company with Janis
     Joplin ("Down on Me")

<u>Key Songs of 1967 in the air that we're still singing</u>:

"All You Need Is Love" - Beatles
"For What It's Worth" - Buffalo Springfield
"You Can't Hurry Love" - The Supremes
"Let's Spend the Night Together" - Rolling Stones
"Respect" - Aretha Franklin
"Sitting on the Dock of the Bay" - Otis Redding
"Brown Eyed Girl" - Van Morrison
"A Whiter Shade of Pale" - Procul Harum
"Dedicated to the One I Love" - The Mamas & The Papas
"Give Me Some Lovin'" - The Spencer Davis Group
"Carrie Ann" - The Hollies
"Girl, You'll Be a Woman Soon" - Neil Diamond
"Ain't No Mountain High Enough" - Marvin Gaye
  & Tammi Terrell
"I Can See for Miles" - The Who

plus...<u>Billboard's 1967 Top 10</u>

1 "To Sir With Love" - Lulu
2 "The Letter" - The Box Tops
3 "Ode to Billie Joe" - Bobbie Gentry

4 *"Windy" - The Association*
5 *"I'm a Believer" - The Monkees*
6 *"Light My Fire" - The Doors*
7 *"Somethin' Stupid" - Frank & Nancy Sinatra*
8 *"Happy Together" - The Turtles*
9 *"Groovin'" - The Young Rascals*
10 *"Can't Take My Eyes Off You" - Frankie Valli*

after a few rounds of this "question-play a few bars of a song" + "question-play a few bars of a song," all songs of guitarist 1's choosing, guitarist 1 simply signals it's time...

guitarist 1:
All of that music was in ONE YEAR, folx...all of it exposing Empire for its cruel ways...all of it revealing the power of Love Itself...all while a war was raging...a war of the Empire's own making....

only love can stop such a thing as Empire in its tracks....

guitarist 1 then plays with gusto the beginning of Jimi Hendrix' "Purple Haze" as they back away into the darkness and EMPIRE (sign) is lowered above the center of the stage and remains there, though under it now appears a subtitle:

Nearly Taking Over Everywhere

— lights fade —

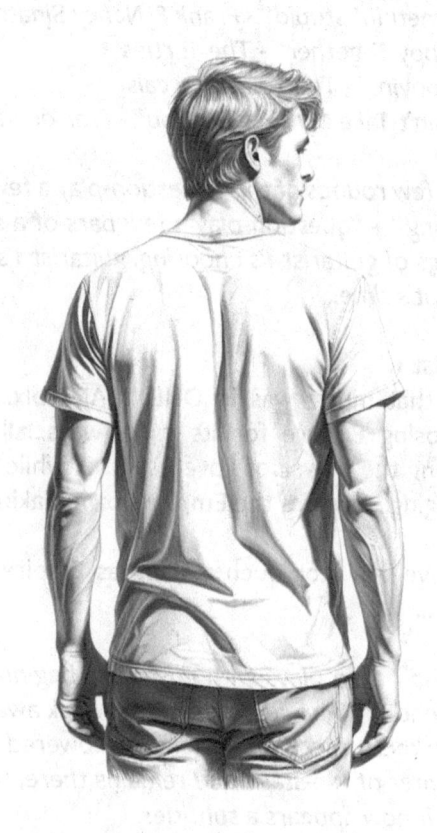

Act 5

— lights up —

owner, *now dressed and acting like a comedic jester in the king's court:*
Well here's the final act, folx, the one you've all been waiting for, and our big super, strong king is here—(*whispers*) to get his oh so tiny dreams interpreted—

(*loudly again*) and here—here—he—comes—folx—

(*king enters, the shortest and least significant of all the players on the stage, he walks on the ground-level like anyone else in his court and has difficulty climbing up onto his throne that sits above the stage at center*)

—our one—our only—
our nation's dearest daddy—the king!

Come on—give him a round of applause, folx—
our very own king!

(*jester agitates the crowd to clap louder and louder*)

king:
Thank you, thank you, my dear, loyal subjects, all of you so much smaller than me down there and yet I

still greet you with all the royal courtesy expected of me—which is none—(*laughs hysterically*)—oh dear, oh dear, oh my very dears, I crack myself up—

jester:
—and us too, my lord, hahahahahaha, us too—so so very funny—hahahaha—and to what do we owe the pleasure of this court today?

king:
Well, funny <u>you</u> should ask as I've had two dreams and no one here in my court has enough stamina to keep up with me—I mean, I mean, no one is brave enough to interpret them—my dreams—

jester:
—oh king—oh dear, dear king—we tried and tried and tried but but—you know—the neverending party here in the royal-court—the hangovers—so hard to think afterwards—I mean—

king:
—silence, slave!

(*as king uses his index finger and thumb to crush jester's head from a distance, repeatedly, maniacally, until king laughs and moves on*)

So I hear that there is someone in my very own dungeon who interprets dreams—I should say—who has the <u>courage</u> to interpret dreams (*as he glares at jester*)—and that you have gussied him all up to stand before me, your most important, most beloved, most powerful king of the universe!

jester:
Yes, my lord, yes we have him all ready for you to, uh, play the part of a prophet, of an ecstatic who can call on the very breath of THE DIVINE—to add up all that you tell him—and—and—here he is folx—he's gonna warm your heart and your—uh—your—uh—give him a warm—a very warm welcome to our dear—foreign—prisoner!!!!

a shaved down or nearly bald Joseph is led out naked by jester to stand with his backside to the audience, front side to the king

king:
Well—oh my dear gods and goddesses—
what do we have here—Jeeeeesuuuuuuus!

king puts a finger in his mouth and and slides it out and then tries to insert his whole hand into his mouth in response to the pleasure-rich sight before him

jester:
King, my dear king—king—king!!—
please—please—be careful—
you do remember the last time you got all excited and tried to put your hand into your mouth—

king:
yesssss—(*exasperated*)—but—but it was nowhere

near as—as—big—and—I mean <u>big</u>—it was—he was—they was—they were—
and you here—you have that <u>and</u> something else down there—now dontcha—you hot—queer—little—I mean HUGE—HUGE thing—

Joseph, *unfazed by the king's questions or lust for him:*
—uh, sir, I understand you've had a dream you'd like interpreted—

king:
—actually two—TWO dreams—as in double the regular size—of dreams—<u>dreams</u>, I tell you—and no one here has had the heart to tell me even a single-serving size of what such a dream could mean—

Joseph:
ah—that's because the interpretation of dreams comes from YAHWEH alone—(*Joseph takes a deep visible breath in and out*)—so let's hear it...

king:
Your dear king dreamed—me!—I did—
—and listen here!—

(*king gets down from his throne with some difficulty, like a toddler trying to find their way down from a chair one foot at a time and begins walking around Joseph*)

I was standing at attention
by The-Great-River-That-Is-Our-National-God
and—listen to this—

out of The-Great-River-That-Is-Our-National-God
seven young bulls were climbing up from the
shore—bulls I tell you—bulls!
(as *king circles around Joseph admiringly*)

They were beautiful looking—
and plump & fat fleshed!
(*king says this while he looks up and down Joseph's
frontside/genitalia*)

And these beautiful bulls were grazing on the
marshy-reeds springing out of our dear divine-
river—divine like me, of course—

and—listen to this—
(as *king walks over toward jester*)
seven more young bulls climbed up after those
beautiful bulls—
right out of The-Great-River-That-Is-Our-National-
God—

these bulls were awful looking—
and their flesh thin & much too lean!

and they were taking their stand near the young,
beautiful bulls on the lip of The-Great-River-That-
Is-Our-National-God—

and the awful looking and lean-fleshed young
bulls <u>ate</u> the seven beautiful looking and plump—
plump!—bulls—
ughhhh!!!—

and then your dear king woke up—
and then one of you slaves soothed me to sleep
again—
you know how I do love a good soothing—
I slept again and dreamed a second time—
and listen here!—
(*all excited...and then kind of bored*)
it was same basic dream
but—but—with corn—
(*all excited again by the imagery/symbolism*)
big—juicy—corn—
(*king walks over to Joseph to get another eye-full, king
tries to put his own hand into his own mouth again*)
and puny little wind-blasted corn—
(*king walks over to jester, spits out his hand, puking,
gagging*)

I woke up in a panic with no one who could soothe
me and no one to tell me the sooth—the truth.
Hahaha, I crack myself up again with my cleverness.

Soothe! Sooth!

Hahahaha—what—what—you don't get my
funny? Look it up, damn it. Look it up, all of you.
(*motioning to the audience too as he shakes his
head with displeasure*) Time to boost our country's
educational standards—

Joseph, *interrupting, with authority and in his fake-
magical voice from earlier when interpreting dreams:*
—ah—your dreams—yes—yes—they are one

dream. Isn't it obvious? (*Joseph turns to jester*)
Seven years—

jester, *spitting mad, interrupting, whispers to
Joseph as king climbs back up onto his throne again,
always with some effort due to his smallish size:*
—well of course it's obvious—but who wants to
give bad news to a fickle king who has a habit of
killing messengers when he's not powerful enough
to control something like a famine??!

(*jester traces his finger up and down Joseph's body
as king keeps looking Joseph up and down and
trying to put his own hand into his mouth*)

But you're cute enough to get away with it—
now aren't you—and you'll probably even get a
promotion doing it—you dirty—little—rascal—

Joseph, *continuing on, speaking to king over
jester's last whispers:*
—seven years of abundance are coming—yes—
and if you're careful and store up and save that
abundance—
with just the right person in charge—
you'll not only survive the seven years of wind-
blasted famine—
you'll save the whole known world—
you'll be known as—<u>the</u>—best—king—ever—
all because (*says hypnotically, fake-magically
like earlier*) you listened to your ecstatic dream-
interpreter and hired him to use this time of

abundance—when—things—like plump bulls—
and plump corn—and every tasty—and juicy
thing—gets—bigger—and—bigger—and—
bigger—and—(*as Joseph uses both hands to
point at what the audience can't see, his genitalia
growing with each word*)

king:
—oh me—oh my dear me—my dear dear me—
how does anyone ever take that—ever get their
mouth and body around all that—<u>you grower</u>—

(*as jester tries to help the nearly faint king back
onto his throne, much like trying to help a toddler*)

—oh dear me—I want my turn on it—I want my—

(*king begins trying to put his whole hand in his
mouth again, with pleasure, and then his other
hand begins reaching around to his own backside,
again with pleasure*)

jester, *trying to wrestle king from pleasuring
himself in public:*
—king—king—my dear king—your royal majesty—
no—not in front of the prisoner—no—no—no—
you cannot act like this in front of someone so
lowly as a prisoner—king—no—stop that—

Joseph, *interrupting, trying to maintain the spell
of the moment that has entranced the king:*
—just remember, king, that you can save your own

kingdom <u>and</u> save the whole known world—and—be—known—as—the—greatest—king—ever—

(*king begins fainting again, this time on top of his throne, jester moves in to support the king and to try to break the spell cast by Joseph upon the king by waving his hands in front of king's eyes fixated on Joseph's erect and diverse genitalia, which the audience cannot see*)

—by selecting someone to be in charge—and sit back and enjoy the fruits of that person's labor—<u>passively</u> (*king gets wildly excited at this word, his hands in his mouth and ass again, jester supporting him*)—you know—be the king by proxy—you know—by elevating this prisoner to King Number Two—

jester *to the hand-to-mouth-and-ass fixated king:*
—you're gonna fall for this, king?

king, *finally pushes jester away:*
I <u>am</u> <u>the</u> <u>king</u>—and I decide—I decide what happens here—and besides—can anyone like this (*points to Joseph*) be found just anywhere—someone who has this much DIVINE breath inside?!

(*king speaks to Joseph and uses one hand to prevent jester from speaking, jester rejects it as dirty—the hand had just been in king's mouth/ass after all*)

And since THE DIVINE has made known this future to you—dearest King Number Two—

you will be over my house—over me—on top of me—
and with your mouth all my people will be kissed—

jester:
—so ridiculously overboard—

king, *still talking to Joseph:*
—and only with the throne will I be greater than you—
you're in charge—of—it—<u>all</u>—

(all said as king descends the throne and removes his ring from his hand and puts it on Joseph's hand)

you are my Number Two *(king himself wraps Joseph in fine clothes that resemble a queen's dress and puts a more masculine gold chain around his neck, genderbending garb which he wears until the end of the play)*

and everyone will call out before you "Kneel!"

so that no one can even attempt to challenge you in raising high their hand or penis <u>or</u> their foot or testicles in our whole land!

— *lights fade, lights up quickly* —

guitarist 1 *sneaks out onstage briefly:*
—and that last line about "kneeling" and "hands and penises" and "feet and testicles"—that's right—check the Hebrew in the Bible—*(smiles, strums the guitar, as he exits)*—if you know, you know!

— lights fade slowly on most of the stage —
(except a small corner)

— EMPIRE sign is elongated —
(to take up almost all of the stage now)

guitarist 1:
Now those seven years of abundance had passed,
and the years of famine following were fierce...
or however many those years really were...
"seven" being a way to say "just right" in the old world...

and thanks to Joseph's foresight, everyone still ate...
except his own family, in a land far away...
(lights come onto them, huddled in the corner)

Jacob *to mob of brothers:*
Why do you stare at each other and do nothing?!
Listen up—I hear that there's food for sale down in
Empire—go on down there and buy some food for
us so that we'll live and not die!

mob of brothers, *in catcall unison:*
<u>Dad</u>—in <u>Empire</u>?!

Jacob:
Go on—I know—I know—
we swore we'd never again cross the border into
any Empire—
but we've driven our car-caravan everywhere but
there—no food anywhere out on the edges—

but there's food there in Empire—
and we're starving—
and as I learned living with my father-in-law, there's
money to be made in any Empire—
it's where the billionaires hang out—
so go on,
get going like the flexible Bordercrossers you are—

(*mob of brothers starts half-heartedly revving their engines with their mouths as they grab youngest brother to join them*)

—all of you but the youngest—I don't want any mischief coming to him as happened to Joseph—

Jacob grabs youngest brother who stays behind with Jacob as mob of brothers crosses the stage revving and exiting, then Jacob exits too

Joseph is highlighted in Empire and dressed as its royalty and youngest brother is highlighted in a land far away in rags worn down by the famine as the revving of the mob of brothers fades offstage

Joseph stands and twirls/dances and youngest brother is drawn to do the same—as if they can see each other, they mimic each other unknowingly and yet all-knowingly—as if seeing each other across the hundreds of miles and remembering each other leading to tears from both and song

Joseph *and* **youngest brother:**

>   You cherish our true nature...
>   The wind is our only friend
>   The wind is our only friend

youngest brother twirls away and exits, mob of brothers enters panting/revving near Joseph

guitarist 1, *while they act it all out:*
And the brothers arrived and bowed down to Joseph.
And Joseph saw his brothers and recognized them—
but he was unrecognizable to them
because of his royal-clothes <u>and</u> all those years—
and he styled it out to them harshly...

Joseph:
From where did you come—
where'd you enter the land?

mob of brothers, *exhaustedly:*
From a land far, far away—
from the land of the Bordercrossers—
the Humble-Traders—the businessmen—to buy food!

guitarist 1:
And Joseph remembered the dreams he'd dreamt
about them...as they all knelt or bowed before him.

He looked around for his youngest brother from
the same mother as him...but didn't find him there.

Joseph, *angrily:*
My sweaty balls! Spies—that's what you are!
To see the land's nakedness—
that's why you've fucking come here, that's why
you fucking entered here!

guitarist 1:
Now in the Biblical Hebrew story's origins, 'balls or
testicles' and 'spies' and 'feet' are all from the same
word—ReGeL.

And the verbs 'to come' and 'to enter' and 'to
fuck'—those are all the same word too—BOAH.
Another version of 'to fuck' like the earlier TaQAY—
in Jacob's wrestling match with YAHWEH.

Wild that original Bible, eh?

mob of brothers, *led by brother 1, echoed by the
others, none of them raising their eyes to Joseph:*
No—my boss—
we're your slaves—
we—we've entered your country to buy food—
all of us are sons of one man—
we are true—
we're your slaves—we aren't spies!

Joseph:
No—the nakedness of the land—
that's what you've all fucking entered to see—
to figure out where to attack us!
Spies! My sweaty balls, you're all spies!!

brother 2, *begging, and Joseph seems to like this begging coming from him:*
All twelve of us—slaves—your slaves—
we are brothers—
sons of one man
from the Humble-Traders'-Land—businessmen—
we're Bordercrossers—wanderers—
and listen here—
the youngest is with our father today—
and one of our younger brothers—he is no more—

Joseph, *playing with them sternly but nearly breaking down crying:*
My sweaty balls! Spies—that's what you are!
In this matter you'll all be tested—
I threaten you by the very life of the king—
if you ever leave here alive—
it'll be because your youngest brother comes here!
To prison you'll all go—
so choose only one of you
to send home to fetch your youngest brother—
while the rest of you'll stay here in prison—
because—by my sweaty balls—you're all spies!

brother 1 and brother 2 fight over who leaves, guitarist 1 continues narrating

guitarist 1:
And Joseph added it all up,
and put them under guard for three days.
And Joseph thought about it all
and said to himself—

Joseph, *aside:*
I'd better not abuse my power
and become The Empire over them....

guitarist 1:
Then he said to them on the third day...

Joseph, *turning back to his brothers:*
Do this and live—
after all I fear the ways of THE DIVINE—
if you are true,
only this one brother of yours'll be imprisoned here,
(points to brother 2, brother 1 is pleasantly surprised)
the rest of you, go and take home food
for the hungry in your houses—
and as for your youngest brother—make him come
here to me—
and that'll prove that you're all trustworthy—
and not spies—and you won't die!

*Joseph runs away from them to the edge of the
stage, overcome with emotion hiding his face*

mob of brothers, *whispering loudly to each other,
each one saying one line to the other:*
Truly we're suffering—
because of what we did to our brother Joseph—
we saw the anguish in his living, breathing body—
when he pleaded with us—
and we didn't listen—
that's why this anguish has come to us now!

Joseph, still on the side of the stage, having overheard

*this, begins weeping, as brother 1 gathers the other
brothers to leave brother 2 in prison, Joseph gets
himself together and personally binds brother 2
right in front of them before the rest of the brothers
exit dejectedly, barely revving as they exit, Joseph
exits the stage looking back at brother 2 with some
fury remembering brother 2 all those years before*

*brother 2 remains on stage in Empire bound in prison
while brothers re-enter and rev back to the smaller
area where Jacob and youngest brother enter*

brother 1 *excitedly to Jacob:*
The man—
one of the royal-bosses of Empire—
he styled it out to us harshly—
he gave it to us like we were spying on Empire—
so we said to him,

> 'We're true—we're honest!
> We're not spies!
> We're twelve brothers—sons of our father!
> One is no more—
> and the youngest is with our father today
> in the land of the Humble-Traders!'

a brother:
Tell Father about the royal-boss's sweaty balls—

brother 1, *trying to override his brother:*
—and then the man—the man—
the royal-boss of the land—he said to us,
> 'By this I'll know that you're true and honest—

you'll lay up one of your brothers with me
and as for the hungry in your house—
take food and go!
Bring your youngest brother to me
and I'll know that you're not spies
and that you are true and honest
and I'll give your brother back to you—
and—and—annnddd—
you'll be able to travel
wherever you want in the land—
and even trade and conduct business here!

mob of brothers, *reacting with surprise at the last bit made up by brother 1, catcall style:*
what?!
wait—did I miss that?
did the man say that?
what a great deal! (*as other brothers hassle this brother about his stupid remark*)

Jacob, *angrily, eventually weeping:*
It's <u>me</u> you miscarry—
(*pauses, looks at them to see if they get it*)
you'll leave me with no children?!
Joseph is no more!
Your brother in Empire's prison won't be much for long!
And my power-son, my youngest son, you're going to take him from me!
My kids are the whole thing! (*he exits dejectedly*)

mob of brothers surrounds youngest brother and revs their engines and takes him off-stage

— lights fade, lights up —

mob of brothers and youngest brother enter revving and get out of their (fake) cars and kneel where Joseph stood and spoke to them earlier, Joseph wears his royal-regalia off to the edge of the stage and watches them and tries to get a glimpse of his youngest brother, brother 2 in prison in another area of the stage

Joseph, *still at the edge of the stage to the manager of his house who enters:*
Take the foreigners to my house—
butcher the meat—
firm things up—
the foreigners will eat with me.

manager's eyes get very large with surprise as he leads mob of brothers and youngest brother a few feet away, then manager fetches brother 2 to join them

manager now curious/suspicious about what will happen moves to the side of the stage and begins washing (pretending) the brothers' junker cars, comedically to watch the action unfold

Joseph enters and brothers all immediately shrivel and bow down to him, though brother 1 has to pull youngest brother to bow down with him because youngest brother is staring at Joseph wide-eyed

Joseph:
Is this your youngest brother—the one you told me about?

no audible response from brothers, in shock

Joseph, *choking back tears, touches youngest brother's cheek:*
May ALL THAT'S DIVINE be gracious to you, my boy!

guitarist 1, *enters over on the edge of the stage, to where Joseph eventually runs overcome with tears:*
And Joseph hurried out of the room—
because they were melting him—
the womb-kindredness he felt for his full brother!

And he wanted so badly to weep—
so he went into his inner-room and wept there.

And he washed his face
and returned back to his brothers
and pulled himself together.

Joseph, *upon returning, loudly to manager:*
Serve the meal!

manager leaves the car-washing to serve the meal, all act out the guitarist's narration

guitarist 1:
And Joseph sat each of the brothers before him—
the oldest where the oldest sits
and the youngest where the youngest sits—

and everyone in the correct order in between—
Joseph knew their birth order and had them sit at
the banquet table with him like that—

of course the brothers were astounded—
and Joseph himself carried royal-sized portions
that were in front of him to them—

and the youngest brother's portion was larger
than anyone else's—five times as large! (*youngest
brother is increasingly taken by Joseph, though he
does not reveal to brothers what he's coming to know*)

And they all drank and got drunk with Joseph.

And as the party rolled on into the night Joseph
pulled aside his manager...

Joseph, *to manager, away from the others:*
Fill up their bags with food—
as much as they can lift—
and put the money each of them paid
inside each bag—
that's right—return their money to them—
and as for my special wine cup—
the valuable, silver one—
put it inside the youngest one's bag
alongside his money from buying food.

guitarist 1:
And the manager of Joseph's house did it all in the
very style that Joseph'd styled out.
And it was morning,

and the men were sent on—
they and their junker cars—
they hadn't even gotten that far—
and Joseph said to his manager...

Joseph *to manager:*
Stand up—
chase after the men—catch them—
and say to them,

> 'Why did you do such bad instead of good?!
> Who stole the very cup that my boss drinks from?!
> He uses that cup
> to hiss like a sacred-snake
> & whisper like the wind—
> he reads the signs
> and tells the future with that cup—
> how could you have done such a stupid thing?!'

guitarist 1:
And Joseph's manager caught up with them
and styled out these very things to them.

mob of brothers, *led by brother 1 as brothers repeat his key phrases:*
Why would my boss style out such things?!
How dare we—your slaves—do something with
such style as this?!!
Whoever is found with my boss's special cup—
<u>he</u> <u>will</u> <u>die</u>—and—we—
the rest of us'll be slaves for my boss forever!"

manager:
Just as you've styled out—let it be so!

each brother opens his bag—oldest to youngest—
brother 1 then brother 2 then onward until
youngest brother, manager examines each bag,
oldest to youngest, until he finds the wine-cup in
youngest brother's bag

brothers all cry and some even tear their clothes out
of exasperation before they load up and return with
manager to Joseph, they fall down at Joseph's feet,
again recalling the dream from earlier and swelling
with tears...though youngest brother is calm

Joseph, *stretching his arms overhead as he did
when brothers stripped him earlier:*
What's this you've done?!
How come you didn't know that I—
a man like me!—
can hiss like a sacred-snake & whisper like the wind—
a man like me!—
can read the signs and tell the future?!

*mob of brothers moans and apologizes over and
over again, everyone except youngest brother who
stands up and keeps staring at Joseph as brother 1
pulls on youngest brother's clothes to get him to
kneel with the rest of the brothers*

Joseph:
To punish you even more—
to add onto your suffering—
I'm keeping your youngest brother here with me—
safe and sound—

and sending the rest of you back home—
to your fath—to your—to your father—

*Joseph can barely get out the last words when he
sees youngest brother taking him in, Joseph quickly
turns his back to them all and weeps*

*youngest brother removes from his pocket a swatch
of Joseph's dress—their mother's dress—that he
kept after Joseph never returned home, youngest
brother brings it to his own nose and inhales,
remembering something more than the dress*

Joseph, *cries out in pain when he glimpses his
youngest brother smelling the dress:*
Make everyone but these foreigners leave me!

*manager and guitarist 1 crowd out to the edges, all
the mob of brothers are still on their knees except
youngest brother who now knows for sure that this
is his brother Joseph and steps toward Joseph as
brother 1 pulls even harder on youngest brother's
clothes to pull him back but youngest brother
reaches out a hand to Joseph who accepts it as
brothers freak out*

Joseph, *at this touch with his youngest brother,
weeps again but recovers enough to sputter this
out to the mob of brothers:*
I'm Joseph!
I'm your brother Joseph.
Is he still—is he—father—is he still alive?

mob of brothers not able to answer him—they tremble, terrified by Joseph, terrified to raise their faces to his face, brother 1 lets go his hold on youngest brother still with the swatch of the dress to his nose steps to embrace Joseph fully

Joseph *to mob of brothers, compassionately, anxiously, says between tears:*
Look here—
your own eyes see—
our youngest brother here knows—he knows—
the way I speak,
my way of styling it out to you—
tell my father all about my weight here—
my respect and honor—
in Empire—tell him all that you've seen—
hurry up—go on—bring my father here right now!

Joseph spoke with such urgency that mob of brothers runs away in the same direction off stage, all we can hear for a moment are the tears of Joseph and his youngest brother—both of them weeping all over one another, until they are soothed by each other and by guitarist 1

guitarist 1, *thoughtfully touching both of their shoulders first, the two weeping in each other's arms as guitarist then plays:*

> You cherish my true nature
> Nothing have I to fear
> No one have I to fear...

(guitarist 1 lets it all hang in the air for awhile...as Joseph and youngest brother continue to hold each other simply and cry quietly in each other's arms...)

Quite a message for our time, yes?

Quite a message for any time, it seems. This story is over two thousand years old.

Joseph—the one stripped by his brothers—reveals himself to his brothers—yet on his own terms.

Revealing oneself, one's true heart—perhaps that's the way of any decent ecstatic—any decent human who lets the Big Wind penetrate them.

(strums a few chords)

Now this is likely the original ending to the story right here—a cliffhanger ending as the prophets are fond of, a cliffhanger-style the real live Jesus used in his parables probably a few hundred years after this Joseph-saga was composed.

A cliffhanger invites us to imagine possibilities.... *(strums)*

Which character bothers you the most? Hmm? Go on, shout it out. *(entertains possibilities)*

You know, a play constellates our guts, right? Kinda like a chessboard with its own rules and logics. We actors move the pieces around for you in a play.

Sometimes a move hurts. Sometimes a character's style of speaking or actions or even existence hurts you or me or your neighbor next to you.

That character that bothers you...how do you change it, make it not hurt?

(*strums guitar for thinking time*)

Ever consider trying love? Send that character who bothers you <u>love</u>...go on...do it right now....

Remember, the songs of the 1960s and 1970's almost transformed a whole world to a new order of love.

It's time again...to cultivate a love that is stronger than hate, than war, than control, than prisons, than concentration camps. It's time again for love.

Ready? Open your heart. Let love rule. Make love with the Divine. Feel YAHWEH feeding you life, befriending you, seeping into you? (*strums and sings*)

> the wind is our truest friend
> the wind is our truest friend

It's been a gift to participate in this ripple of love with all of you here today/tonight.

guitarist 1 begins bowing as if the show is over but Jacob and mob of brothers enter stage, much to the surprise of guitarist 1...

Jacob embraces Joseph as they both weep, and youngest brother joins them in the embrace. Jacob then looks to the mob of brothers who brought him to Joseph....Joseph regards them, unsure what to do, brothers 1 & 2 are whispering behind the mob with their backs to the group as brother 1 pulls out a large knife from his clothes...Jacob comes and finds them as brother 2 hurriedly hides the knife in his clothes... Jacob leads brothers 1 & 2 to kneel before Joseph, other mob/brothers kneel behind brothers 1 & 2

guitarist 1, *as all of this unfolds:*
Well, I thought we'd found a nice ending here with Joseph and his youngest brother...their beautiful tears and all....but looks like this family wants to let this story play out a little further, past the cliffhanger....

brother 1, *speaking with sarcasm to Joseph, as brother 2 reaches into his clothes for the knife:*
You gave up all your songs—your so strong and beautiful ideals—to serve the <u>Empire</u>?!

Joseph, *matching the sarcasm:*
Some of us have to do whatever we can—even if it means seducing the king—to get out of the prisons our brothers throw us into—

brother 2 pulls the knife from his clothes—there's an audible gasp from those who can see this on stage—brother 2 considers stabbing Joseph but notices manager moving in quickly to defend Joseph—brother 2 panics and presents the knife to Joseph in deference

Joseph, *throwing the knife offstage, shouting:*
For crying out loud, brothers, when will you stop these ridiculous games?!! *(brothers 1 & 2 cower)*

brother 2, *says as brother 1 tries to get away from brother 2 to make it appear he wasn't involved:*
Are you going to kill us??!

Joseph, *wildly angry, his arms overhead like earlier:*
What you did to me all those years was flat out wrong—all of you brothers—for years *(his anger giving over to tears, arms drop)*—such hatred—just because—because I'm different—I was so young and figuring it all out *(weeps)*—just a very different boy trying to add it all up—you made my life hell—<u>hell</u>!!— *(weeps again, youngest brother holds him more tightly)*

brother 1, *grabbing brother 2's clothes and trying to get brother 2 to join his apology:*
—we are sorry—we're so so sorry—we had no idea what would happen—all—all this—

Joseph:
—but—but the breeze of life rushed upon me—carried me forward—all the way here—all the way to the Number Two position—Number Two to the king himself—

brother 2:
—please don't kill us, Joseph! Please!!!!

Joseph:
The king would think nothing of my killing you.
(*pauses*) But no. I'm not going to kill you.

brother 2:
Are you going to put us in prison?

Joseph:
If prisons were designed for reforming people—
maybe. But the king and all too many of his subjects
want their prisons to be punishment—no matter
how much I intervene—

mob of brothers:
—are you going to torture us?
—take our cars? our money?
—get your revenge on us?

Joseph, *getting an idea:*
Maybe I put you to work researching new prison
models...prisons that provide opportunities for
prisoners to reform themselves...like the ones
Germany has now in the 21st century—(*turns to the
audience*) that's right, check it out—**_Germany_**—
even with their tragic 100-year history—Germany
leads the world in prison reform—

mob of brothers, *catcall-style again to Joseph:*
—are you forcing us to do this work?
—weilding your new power over us?
—as punishment?

Joseph:
No. I'm giving you a job. A chance. Who better to want prison reform than people who should be there themselves.

mob of brothers:
What???!

Joseph:
It's what any family or any society does with its so-called "least" that says the most.

brother 1, *with echoes from the others:*
But what are we supposed to know about prison reform?! yeah? huh?

Joseph:
Shine some light upon the ugliness in our family.
We are Abraham's descendants—<u>Abraham</u>—
our primal bordercrosser whose story gave birth
to Judaism, Christianity, Islam.

As you know, terrible things have been done to us
for centuries as Abraham's children;
and we as Abraham's children have done terrible
things to each other and to others.

mob of brothers:
Terrible things?! We didn't do terrible things—

Joseph:
—you brothers committed genocide within a town
to avenge our sister's rape—you've forgotten?!?

guitarist 1 *to audience:*
Uh, we skipped <u>that</u> Bible story today...but you could look it up: Genesis 34.

brother 2, *shocked that Joseph would bring it up, with catcalls from the other brothers in support:*
But Joseph, that guy raped our sister—

Joseph:
—and then you brothers <u>killed</u> <u>the</u> <u>whole</u> town—not just him! Disgusting!

brother 2:
They made themselves our enemies!

Joseph:
The <u>children</u> you killed—they were your enemies? The people who had nothing to do with the guy who raped our sister—they were your enemies?

(pauses for understanding)

Look, we can be kings over each other, over anyone, and mete out punishments and control every move...

or, <u>or</u>, **_or_**

(moves to the other side of the stage to say these next lines)

we can be bordercrossers who know we're all in this life together....

(*gesturing to everyone on stage and everyone in the audience*)

What do you choose—which imagination, which style?

I know it seems ridiculous coming from me, as I stand here as the king's Number Two...but we all do what we gotta do in the circumstances in which we find ourselves....

(*pauses again for understanding*)

Maybe a real bordercrossing imagination would get the playwright to add some decent lines for the silent-characters in this play!

cast & crew from onstage and offstage—*everyone but the mob of brothers, all catcalling:*
yeah!
right!
heck yeah!

Rachel, *in dress, loudest, entering stage:*
About time, damn it!

manager, *highfiving Rachel:*
Damn right!

mob of brothers, *shocked by this outcry:*
But Joseph—once we reform the prisons, will you put us in there?

Joseph:
Your job is to make sure that life inside prison and life outside prison—that both are equally healthy for all—

mob of brothers:
—but Joseph—there are murderers in there—bad people who do terrible things—

Joseph:
—you mean like yourselves?

mob of brothers, *confused:*
But Joseph—

Joseph:
—you killed a whole town for one person's action!! Our own father protested what you did! (*Jacob nods yes*)

mob of brothers:
But Joseph—

Joseph:
—brothers—family—we can't keep closing our hearts to our complicated history. Keep doing that and history becomes systemic, and comes around even more nastily each time—

mob of brothers:
—but Joseph—

Joseph:
—the one who opens their heart to everyone in the system changes the whole system,
the whole family,
the whole society,
the whole history,
the whole world.

mob of brothers:
But Joseph—

Joseph:
—brothers, begin a revolution for all humanity—
(*pauses*)

let it begin with us (*pleading*)—
all of us from the family who gave birth to Judaism, Christianity, and Islam!

mob of brothers:
But Joseph—

Joseph, *more sternly at first but softening:*
—or go home to the famine and take your chances there. But here there is food. And safety. And a job. And a place for you and your families to settle. A place to breathe and live and grow.

breeze blows from offstage, each person feels it in their own way, soothes the situation, brings smiles, guitarist 2 and all cast/crew assemble on stage

guitarist 1, *noticing the wind and responding to it:*
Show's about to end here in a few minutes, folx.

And after it does, please do find a few new friends in the lobby.

Talk about what happened for you here today/tonight.

guitarist 2:
Take the conversations into the bars and cafes—revive those places where shared freedom was first imagined by our ancestors—all over Earth.

Share your thoughts on the global stage too—the internet could help us.

guitarist 1:
Change begins with the Average Joes like you and me. *(strums a few more chords from the song)* Well, we're not so average, right?

guitarist 2:
Until that day when we realize we are all One in this same air, this same life-giving breeze...

(in place of EMPIRE sign, these lyrics below could run for the audience to join in easily, cast/crew hand in hand, arm in arm, as one family, possibily including audience if it feels right, as all sing:)

Dancing under a new moon
The breeze is our truest friend
The breeze is our truest friend

You cherish our real nature
Nothing have we to fear
No one have we to fear

Dancing under a new moon
The breeze is our truest friend
The breeze is our truest friend...

song repeats as needed
until a guitarist signals for it all to end together

— as song concludes, final bow, curtain —

a note about the song...

It's my hope that a songwriter in any and every dramatic circle staging this play will compose music that works with these lyrics for their circle of dramatic-ecstatics.

It's also my hope that each circle's version of the song is different musically from the others. Same or very similar words, different music. Let creativity and possibility thrive.

Let the revolution (re)commence....

an addendum, if needed:

If guitarists face any challenges with the audience anytime during the show, especially during the audience participation portions, they could say something like this to the person(s)...

guitarist:
Sounds like you have a lot of feeling about this. And that's important to listen to, for us all to listen to. I wonder, though, if your argument is really with the Bible and God—more than it is with us.

(*if more is needed*) You might want to have a conversation with God and why God would allow this ___ (*whatever person protests*) in the Bible, in life. And take some inspiration from the Jacob and YAHWEH wrestling story...just be ready for what YAHWEH likes to do with Its challengers...(*laughs*)... did you bring some lube for yourself, or YAHWEH? Wrestling with YAHWEH has Its rewards, after all.

And remember you are free to stay or go—no one is forcing you to stay here...and besides, all of these fine people have paid to be here too.

And I suspect words like these will be heard differently coming from someone standing there naked (or in swimsuit/underwear) with a guitar.

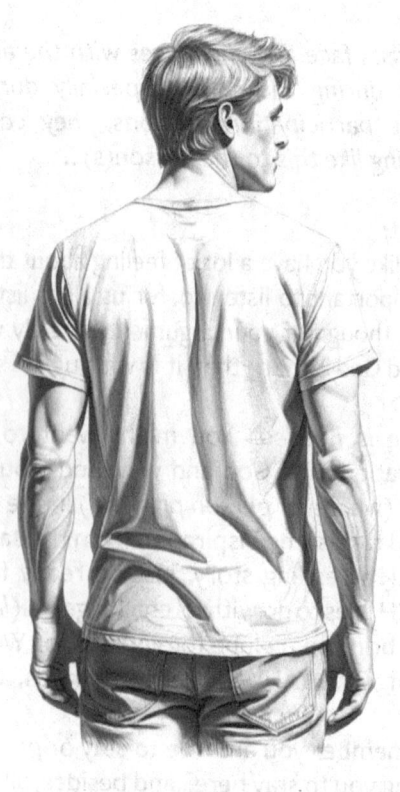

Bible Translation Fragment:
Jacob wrestling

Joseph's wrestling-with-God dream in *No Average Joseph* is based on Genesis 32.

As the plot thickens in the story of Joseph's father Jacob...just after Jacob had wriggled free of the argument with his father-in-law and just as Jacob discovers his once-murderously-angry brother is coming at him with 400 men—definitely not a welcoming party!—Jacob divides up all he has into a few batches of gifts to assuage his brother Esau, whose name means "do it"—possibly "done roughly." Despite YAHWEH's promises to protect Jacob, Jacob plans to hide from his brother's entourage in the last batch—not exactly showing trust in YAHWEH.

And where is Jacob and his family as they prepare to confront "do it rough" Esau? In Seir. Satyr... those furry, devilish little creatures. Seir and Satyr are from the same linguistic root...and also a word to describe a storm that rages out of nowhere, a tempest, the terrified trembling that Nature has a way of bringing forth in us humans as we confront how quickly our lives can be taken from us by wind and storm and sea...the very forces that also give us life.

Where in Seir? By a little branch of the Jordan River...the Going-Down-River...a branch named Demoralize-and-Devastate. (!)

And what of that crossing-place Demoralize-and-Devastate? Imagine a creek that seems tame and pleasant and then all of the sudden can swell with deadly force...something too many in our world know today too.

Spooky. Terrifying. Deadly.

And out of nowhere in this middle-of-nowhere place, some "rando" shows up to wrestle.

If the rough hair/fur on the back of your neck is not yet standing up...it will in a moment!

This story is an excellent example of something that was most certainly performed out loud in the ancient world. How would we know that? Listen to the repeated sounds and note how they play with shades of meaning here...how the narrative then swirls with even more playful possibilities...based on sounds...

YaBaQ/AHBaQ/YAYQaB
...plus another hard-Q sound and pivotal word of the story: TaQAY

'bordercross'/AYBaR - used 6 times in this small chunk of the story below as verb or noun and very similar in sound to the primal bordercrosser in the biblical tradition, Abraham/AHBRaHaM (bordercrossers/Hebrews = AYBaRYM)

'because, surely'/KY - used often, often with different shades of meaning

plus a few other playful gems you'll discover below...food for one's ears and one's imagination, ancient or today! Try sounding out the Biblical Hebrew words when they come up in the story and catch more of the cleverness of the story....

A more careful translation of Genesis 32:21-31 found in the Bible, about Jacob, Joseph's far from average father:

And the gift/MeNCHaH (for his brother Esau) was bordercrossed on ahead of him (over to the other side of the border/river)—
and he stayed that night in the camp/MeCHeNaH, perhaps even stayed there stubbornly.

And he stood up tall that night,
and took his two wives and his two maid-slaves and his eleven boys/children,
and bordercrossed over the bordercrossing-place of the Demoralize-and-Devastate/YaBaQ—

he took them and bordercrossed them over the creek-bed (which can also mean "inheritance/

possessions")—he bordercrossed over what was his—"his possessions, his family."

And Jacob/YAYQaB remained there all by himself.

And he kicked up the dust and wrestled/AHBaQ—

a man with him—

until dawn climbed up—

and he saw that he wouldn't be able to hold his own with him—

and he groped the hollow of his thigh and genitals—his ass—

and the hollow of Jacob's thigh and genitals—his ass—was impaled—banged—fucked/TaQAY—
in kicking up the dust and wrestling with him/AHBaQ!

And he said,
"Let me loose—
because the dawn's climbing up!"

And he said,
"No, I won't let you loose—
because—surely—you'll bring me into abundance!"

And he said to him,
"What's your name?"

And he said,
"Jacob/YAYQaB!"

And he said,
"Not Jacob/YAYQaB!
Your name won't be called that anymore—
because—surely—you are Israel—
which means On-Top-of-God—
because you've been topping THE DIVINE and
humans and have held your own!"

And Jacob/YAYQaB asked—he said,
"Tell me—please—your name!"

And It said,
"Why this—why do you ask for my name?!"

And It offered him the abundance of life, right there.

And Jacob/YAYQaB called out the name of the place,

"Divinity's-Face!
because I've seen THE DIVINE—faces to faces!—
and my living, breathing body was stripped
away—snatched away alive/NaTSeL!"

And It shown brightly on him—the sun did—
just as he bordercrossed through Divinity's-Face—

and he'd been ribbed-and-limping/TSLAY because
of his thigh and genitals and ass.

* * * *

In the spirit of cliffhangers, perhaps we can leave it right here for now...

My scholarly friends will be quick to point out that the Abraham and Isaac and Jacob and Joseph stories are all disparate tales from very different centuries all united into a sweeping, somewhat unified, somewhat messy, as-if-it's-a-four-generation-saga in the Torah. (See Römer.)

The Joseph portion was probably the last to be added and woven into the Genesis scroll.

Yes. Agreed. I appreciate my scholarly-minded friends zooming out to help us all see this.

My scholarly friends living today could benefit by becoming more poetically-minded and zooming into the terrain of the language and noticing the peculiarities present—and the jaw-dropping word choices and playful, similar-sounding words. (See Jennings.)

Not much of these ancient tales makes sense unless the Biblical Hebrew is read out loud. After all, most of these tales were likely conceived and shared orally and later written down, sometimes much later. Reading the Biblical Hebrew out loud is the only way to catch the clevernesses that happen within one's mouth in nibbling upon and savoring the tasty fruit of the received text. (See Shircliff.)

By the way, the limping-wound Jacob is experiencing hearkens back to Adam's, the fictional-mythical-ancestor set up in the Genesis-saga to be first mud-creature-human of the bordercrossing band of these YAHWEH-inspired-and-inspiring ecstatics, these storycrafters who first told these stories in these dusty lands of Israel and Judah (the Levant) as they tried to slip free from the cruel empires of Assyria, Babylon, and Ancient Egypt...to name a few. Empires must have enemies...it gives them something to do, someone to circle, someone to threaten, someone to swallow. Empires and hierarchies—be they national or corporate or even religious—are sick systems for adults to enact upon each other. They do not let us feel and decide for oneself, personally or communally/circularly.

The Biblical Hebrew word for 'rib' and this kind of 'limping' Jacob experiences are rather strangely (from) the same Hebrew word...TSLAY. Brings a whole new meaning to "slaying it."

And then the word with even more oomph... TaQAY/'banged, nailed, fucked'...!

Let YAHWEH/breath in or die, after all.

Wrestle well, friends.

Resources for the Journey

on YAHWEH as the old wind/storm divinity honored by the wandering Shasu people:
> *The Invention of God*. Thomas Römer. Cambridge, MA: Harvard, 2015.

on how the Hebrew Bible was put together:
> anything by Thomas Römer, many short books in French and English, many videos on YouTube

on Joseph and his dress:
> *Jacob's Wound: Homoerotic Narrative in the Literature of Ancient Israel*. Theodore W. Jennings Jr. New York: Continuum, 2005. In this book we can see scholars going from 'it couldn't possibly be a dress in the Joseph story' to 'the dress actually works in the story.' Yes!

on more of the clever style of the Hebrew text with the Joseph story and throughout Genesis:
> *A Wildly Sensual YAHWEH: The Controversial Genesis Stories in the Bible* (vol 0 of *The Naked Path of Prophet* series). Brian J. Shircliff. Cincinnati: VITALITY, revised 2024.

on humans who helpfully blow up our gender constructs:
> *XXY* (movie, 2007)

"The one who opens their heart to everyone in the system changes the whole system"...Brian heard Stephan Hausner say something similar in a Constellations workshop in Asheville, August 2024.

About the Playwright & Translator

In addition to *The Naked Path of Prophet* series and now *Naked Little Fictions*, Brian Shircliff is the poet of *winds of (r)evolution* (paintings by Matthew Klooster) and author of the graphic novel *YAHWEH IS THE WIND!* (illustrated by Sean K. Long). Having taught high school religion for seventeen years, he felt the need to swim away from the shipwreck of organized religion for a more inclusive perspective, where the wind blows freely and surprisingly. He is a Bones for Life® Trainer, Guild Certified Feldenkrais Practitioner®, Healing Touch Certified Practitioner, and thirty-year student of many styles of meditation, tai chi, and yoga. He co-founded and continues to direct VITALITY Cincinnati's donation-based holistic self-care programs.

Brian usually hires artists to create images for his books, an opportunity to spread their important creative work. It seemed wiser and safer with our world politics to use Canva images for this cover.

About Licensing This Play

Reach out to Brian by calling VITALITY's phone number listed on **vitalitycincinnati.org**.

Licensing fees help VITALITY grow affordable, holistic, self-awakening programs in-person in Cincinnati and via Zoom around the world.

VITALITY

growing love,
sharing holistic self-care,
and inspiring creative expression.

We invite you to explore with us through our
affordable, friendly drop-in classes...
in person & online

vitalitycincinnati.org

and our books

vitalitybuzz.org

www.ingramcontent.com/pod-product-compliance
Lightning Source LLC
Chambersburg PA
CBHW010939120626
46554CB00008B/2537